Requiem for
a Lawnmower

By Sally Wasowski
with Andy Wasowski

Native Texas Plants:
Landscaping Region by Region

Requiem for a Lawnmower

AND OTHER ESSAYS ON EASY GARDENING WITH NATIVE PLANTS

Sally Wasowski

With Andy Wasowski

TAYLOR PUBLISHING COMPANY
DALLAS, TEXAS

This book is printed on recycled paper.

Frontispiece: Mexican Hat *(Ratibida columnaris)*
Illustrations by Susan Edison

Published by Taylor Publishing Company
          1550 West Mockingbird Lane
          Dallas, Texas 75235

Designed by David Timmons

Library of Congress Cataloging-in-Publication Data

Wasowski, Sally, 1946–
    Requiem for a lawnmower : and other essays on easy gardening with
native plants / Sally Wasowski with Andy Wasowski.
      p. cm.
    ISBN 0-87833-811-X
    1. Native plant gardening—United States. 2. Landscape gardening—
United States. I. Wasowski, Andy, 1939–   . II. Title.
SB439.W38 1992
635.9′5173—dc20   92-10980
                                                            CIP

Printed in the United States of America
10 9 8 7 6 5 4 3 2 1

Acknowledgments

I would like to thank the following people for helping me with information on grasses and prairie flowers:

John Clegg, Arlington, Texas
Dan James, Western Sere, Casa Grande, Arizona
Scott Stewart, ConservaSeed, Rio Vista, California
Cathy Macdonald, Oregon Natural Heritage Database, Portland, Oregon

Contents

Introduction   *3*

Going Back to Basics

Stop Fighting Mother Nature   *11*

All.or Nothing?   *15*

When a Native Isn't   *18*

Zeroing in on Your Own Backyard

Taking a Regional View   *23*

Provenance Is Not a City in Rhode Island   *26*

Danger in Your Bookstore   *29*

Good People, Good Intentions, Bad Input   *32*

Be the First Person on Your Block to
   Have an Ecologically Sound Landscape   *36*

Can You Say Xeriscape?   *41*

Better Things for Better Living
   Through . . . Organic?   *44*

Putting It All Together

Requiem for a Lawnmower   *49*

So You Think You Can Landscape a
   Garden, Huh?   *53*

Made for the Shade   *58*

How to Keep from Killing Your Wooded Lot   *61*

Don't Let Your Wildflowers Run Wild   *66*

Transplanting Made Easy *68*

A Yaupon Holly Is Not a Lollypop! *75*

Leave Those Leaves *79*

A Native for Every Niche

. . . And So to Bedding *83*

Cenizo . . . Recognition at Last! *87*

Grass Roots Support for Buffalograss *90*

Mexican Hat: A Black-thumb Perennial *96*

Putting Ferns in Their Proper Place *98*

Sumacs for Red Fall Color *104*

Our Unsung Horticultural Heroes *108*

Observations

Rediscovering Our Lost Native Herbs *115*

Watch the Birdies Instead of the Soaps *121*

Things That Go Bump in the Spring *124*

Fast Food Stops for Hummingbirds *126*

Goldenrod Is Nothing to Sneeze At *129*

Trash Trees: Mother Nature's Band-Aids *131*

Creating Habitats

How Natural Is Natural? *137*

Create Your Own Woods *141*

Little Prairie by the House *146*

A Kinder, Gentler Desert Garden *152*

Mother Nature's Winter Garden *157*

Looking for a Good Neighbor? Try a Creek. *160*

The Floating Bladderwort *167*

Where Do We Go from Here?

The Eighth Deadly Sin   *172*

Where Have All the Saplings Gone,
    Long Time Passing?   *176*

To Save the Planet, Save the Plants   *179*

For
Sara and Sophie

Our Mothers

Introduction

Your lawn looks great," she said.

"Great? This belongs in a magazine. I've never seen a puttin' green look this good. I deserve garden of the month, but they won't give it to me . . . Wrong part of town. It always goes to those rich folks who hire yard boys to do all the work while they sit by the pool and sip daiquiries. It does look good, doesn't it?"

"It's incredible. How many times a week do you mow?"

"Three or four."

JOHN GRISHAM
The Firm

**Cedar Waxwing and
Possumhaw Holly**
Ilex decidua

Most people go through their entire lives without a single epiphany. I've had two.

The first one happened on September 27, 1980, and I have my mother to thank for it. She called me up one day and told me about a gardening seminar she'd heard about. "You'd probably enjoy it," she said. "It has to do with landscaping with those wildflowers you're so crazy about."

In fact, as it turned out, that seminar dealt with far more than wildflowers; it introduced me to a whole new category of plants: natives! I heard for the first time the startling news that one could landscape with a wide repertoire of natives; not just wildflowers, but shade trees, ornamental trees, groundcovers, shrubs, vines . . . as well as perennials and annuals in staggering varieties. This was—and still is—a fairly radical notion for traditional gardeners, which I was at that time.

That seminar presented an impressive array of speakers, all of whom had grown, collected, and selected native plants with a horticultural eye. Two speakers in particular, Carroll Abbott and Benny J. Simpson, were *so* inspiring that they literally changed the direction of my life.

From then on, whenever and wherever they spoke in the area, I was there—just like a jazz fan going to hear Ella, or a Trekkie off to meet Leonard Nimoy. When I heard that both were going to be guest lecturers at a landscaping course at Texas Woman's University, I got permission to leave work early every Friday so I could drive to Denton to take their classes.

I should point out that I was not professionally involved in landscaping at that time; I was a social worker. But I'd always had a love affair with gardening. Some of my fondest memories are of my Grandmother Hudson leading me by the hand around her garden. And, no matter where I've lived— Texas, New York, Virginia, Illinois—I've always had a flower garden, composed primarily of plants I've scrounged out of alleys or vacant lots. These were, of course, native and some naturalized flowers, although I didn't even know those terms then. Yet I think I knew instinctively that these hardy blooms would do well for me. You see, the truth is, despite my love of flowers, I'm simply not willing to devote the many hours it takes to keep more finicky flora looking their best.

Until that seminar, my interest in gardening had been very casual and largely unfocused. Certainly, I had never considered making it a career. I was a plant collector, rather than a designer, and I strolled around in my garden the way I still visit museums, taking in just one thing at a time. And, even though I'd had art training in college, it had never occurred to me that I might actually design a landscape of my own, let alone for paying clients.

Those gardens that I'd had back then were already established when I moved in; I had just puttered with them a bit, trying something here, something else there. In New York I once added dozens of feet of flower beds to the existing plot, but they were all in straight, narrow lines around the perimeter of the lawn. This was how my grandmother had done it; it wasn't very creative or aesthetically rewarding, but it sure made weeding easier. As I said, traditional.

I've always considered a garden an outside room, a place to sit in and watch the sun go down, or to have a picnic in, or a nook to lounge and read, surrounded by sweet scents and the hum of bees. I certainly never considered a garden as a place to put in a lot of hard work, watering and weeding and dead-heading. And, especially, mowing! In other words, what I'd always dreamed of was a garden that required as little effort as possible.

Until that seminar, that's all it was, a dream. But suddenly, here were these people telling me that what I'd been looking for all my life was possible. I really could have plants that virtually took care of themselves, *beautiful* plants that didn't demand that I devote all of my spare time to their welfare. Using native plants, I quickly realized, meant that gardening was no longer dependent on how far the garden hose could reach or how big a water bill one was willing to endure.

As I said, my life changed directions. I began to learn all that I could about these marvelous native plants. And Benny Simpson, a kind and generous gentleman, became my mentor, guru, and treasured friend.

Eventually, I found the nerve to actually try my hand at a few landscape designs for people other than myself, first for family members and then—miracle of miracles—for a few brave souls who were actually willing to pay to be guinea pigs. I didn't charge them very much at first because my work wasn't worth very much. In fact, I thought I might be downright dangerous.

Old ideas die hard. Looking back, I now realize that I made many mistakes because I still thought in traditional terms; almost all of the unsuccessful plants I put in were from standard-issue nursery stock. Of course, those same mistakes were being made every day by "real" professionals. They still are! And those native plants that I was experimenting with turned out to be my triumphs.

As for that second epiphany, well, that happened over a lunch about five years later. Dayton Reuter, a professor at the University of Texas at Arlington and a talented landscape architect, had seen my first book, *Landscaping with Native Texas Plants,* a book I wrote for the simple reason that I needed such a resource in my landscaping business and none existed. My landscape plans in that book represented pretty innovative ideas for the time—a woods in the front yard, a bird garden, and a patio garden with no lawn—but I was still thinking of native plants as substitutes for standard gardening fare.

Dayton had been trained in the traditions of that Midwestern genius, Jens Jensen, who in the early decades of the twentieth century started using native plants to recreate prairie and woodland habitats.

With the gentle tact found in truly gifted teachers, Dayton made me realize how rigid my thinking still was, and he taught me to think of plants not just as individuals, but as integral parts of a plant community. Moreover, for these plants to succeed as a community, they must all be native, or indigenous, to the same site, such as your property, and not merely native to a political unit, such as the state you live in.

It was as if he'd flipped on the light switch in a dimly lit room. Suddenly, I understood that I was free to toss aside traditional thinking and create truly natural landscapes, real woods and prairies, for example, where all the plants are indigenous and arranged so that they relate to each other as they do in nature. After all, these natives have evolved together, so they already know how to grow together in harmony. A whole new world of design ideas had been opened up for me.

————————

People often ask me about my qualifications for doing landscape design. I patiently explain that, no, I am not a landscape architect; that is a degreed professional who deals primarily with the construction aspects of landscaping. Surprisingly, very little of that training is devoted to plant materials. And, of that, almost none deals with native plants. Dayton Reuter, and a handful of other LAs I've met, are the exceptions, not the rule.

Landscape designers, at least the ones I know, are, first and foremost, plant people. They are artists who often come from a variety of backgrounds. It is not unusual for a landscape designer and a landscape architect to combine their skills; I've worked that way many times.

I have found that my lack of formal training in either landscape design or standard horticulture has, for the most part, been an asset. Because I was free of the dogmas with which, I feel, many university-trained professionals get saddled, I was able to grasp Dayton's ideas without feeling like a heretic. Without any formal schooling in landscaping, I was able to examine *all* of the possibilities; I wasn't hampered by preconceived notions of what was right or wrong.

Because of my second epiphany with Dayton Reuter, I began observing entire plant communities and recreating them in semi-civilized forms in the gardens I designed.

The more I observed, the more I realized that plant communities were habitats, and that plants, animals, soil, water, and rocks all logically and naturally fit together. This led inescapably to a closer look at what is happening to our land, our water supplies, and our ecology. And, I came to believe that watering, fertilizing, poisoning, and other ways in which

Monarda with
Pipevine Swallowtail
Monarda fistulosa

we manipulate nature are extravagances that will not be options for us in the future. I'm convinced that we need to completely change our whole approach to gardening.

We need to look at the basics again and see how Mother Nature, the best gardener of all, has managed these many millennia. The more I learn about her, the more she fascinates, teaches, and inspires me.

Frequently, I'm asked to give talks about native plants. It's exciting to address a crowd of several hundred native plant enthusiasts. But, whenever I do, I have to remind myself that, outside that auditorium, there are many thousands of people in that town who don't have any idea what native plants are, or what they can do.

There's still a lot of educating to do, a lot of eyes left to be opened. This book is a small attempt to reach those of you who still haven't heard the good news—or, having heard, now want to know more. I know, that makes me sound like a missionary, but that's okay; that's how I feel sometimes. I am a botanical missionary. And, I love it when some homeowner comes up to me and says, "You know, I started using native plants a few years ago, and you're right, they're terrific! Thanks!"

The title of this book reflects another significant comment I hear very often from my audiences. When I describe the more natural landscape designs that natives make possible, I invariably see row after row of broad grins breaking out, followed by a chorus of disbelieving voices—male and female—saying, "You mean we won't have to mow anymore?"

Special note: This book is intended for people all over the United States—even up into Canada—so I've tried to tell my story with as broad a basis as possible. I live and work here in Texas, however, so some of the examples I use and the people I refer to are ones I know from firsthand experience. In those cases, be assured, the basic ideas and principles I'm talking about will apply just about everywhere.

So read and enjoy. And who knows? Maybe this book will trigger an epiphany for you.

Dallas, Texas
December, 1991

Going Back to Basics

If dandelions were rare and fragile, people would knock themselves out to pay $14.95 a plant, raise them by hand in greenhouses, and form dandelion societies and all that. But they are everywhere and don't need us and kind of do what they please. So we call them "weeds," and murder them at every opportunity.

ROBERT
FULGHUM
*All I Really Need
To Know I Learned
·In Kindergarten*

Let us permit nature to have her way; she understands her business better than we do.

MICHEL DE
MONTAIGNE

**Buff-Bellied Hummingbird
and Coral Honeysuckle**
Lonicera sempervirens

Stop Fighting Mother Nature

⤳

Ever wonder why there are so many weekend gardening shows on the air all over the country? Or, why the gardening section of your bookstore is becoming almost as crowded as the shelves devoted to cookbooks?

The implication seems to be that gardening is an incredibly tough undertaking. Not only do we need an army of experts to advise and guide us, but we also must put forth herculean efforts: pruning, weeding, watering, and mowing if we want our landscapes to survive and look pretty. And, we have to spend tons of money at our neighborhood nurseries and garden supply centers: for seeds, replacement plants that seem to die at an alarming rate, and all of those chemical fertilizers and bug sprays.

Conventional gardening—the type practiced by the vast majority of American homeowners—calls for just this sort of all-out effort. And, the reason is simple: *To a great degree, we are fighting Mother Nature. We are doing it the hard way.*

Fellow gardeners, I have good news for you. It doesn't have to be that way!

Believe it or not, your garden can look terrific all year with minimum upkeep and no toxic chemicals at all. All you have to do is start relying on those wonderful native plants that Mother Nature put in your area thousands and thousands of years ago. That's what makes a plant a native: it has been around for so long that it has learned how to cope with the unique conditions in your area.

Do you live in a part of the country that gets just a few begrudging inches of rain each year? The local native plants do just fine with picayune amounts of water that would kill your average nursery flora. And, if you live in coastal wetlands, with annual downpours that seem to encourage ark-building, be assured that the native plants that evolved in your region are quite happy with all of that moisture.

Do you live on acid soil? The native plants in your area thrive on acid. Do you have surprise spring freezes? You can't fool the local native plants; they've learned how to wait out the weather, and they start blooming only when the warm weather has come to stay.

Landscaping with native plants is just plain common sense. It's working *with* Mother Nature, not against her.

Why was it not until the 1970s that we started awakening to this fact? Why have native plants taken a backseat to imported varieties for so long? Let's take a quick history lesson:

When European settlers came to this land centuries ago, they had their hands full just surviving. They had to cope with harsh weather, swamp fever, and ongoing conflicts with Native American tribes that understandably were not terribly thrilled about being pushed off their land by these pale-faced strangers. Whatever gardening these settlers were doing was limited to coaxing a few crops out of the ground so they could eat.

Eventually, of course, life got easier for them. Three square meals a day became pretty standard fare, and our forebears looked around one day and realized that their hard-scrabble frontier existence was becoming, well, civilized.

Now it was possible for them to garden for pleasure, not just for food. Naturally, these settlers wanted their new gardens to *look* civilized. And where were the most civilized gardens they knew? Why, back home, of course—where they'd come from, England and Northern Europe.

So, they imported seeds and saplings from the Old World and planted their new gardens with flowers and shrubs that had evolved elsewhere: Cedar of Lebanon, English boxwood, and flowers such as hollyhocks and carnations. No consideration was given to whether or not these imported plants would like their new home. In many cases, they did not. The settlers tried to convince the plants that Georgia wasn't really a whole lot different from Nottingham or Leeds, but the plants weren't buying.

But never mind, one simply ordered new plants. The companies that shipped the European plant stock to the New World must have got filthy rich on reorders.

As for all of the colorful and hearty native flowers, trees, shrubs, vines, and groundcovers that were thriving all about—right under the very noses of the settlers—well, these were considered weeds, hardly fit company for the imports. The exceptions were a few natives such as delphinium and Virginia creeper that had been shipped off to European gardens, where they were cultivated, hybridized, and were shipped right back again.

In all fairness, it's hard to blame those settlers for their snobbish attitude toward the native plants. The natives, you see, were growing wild and uncared for. Naturally, they didn't look their best. Listen, if you were living out in a field, with no one to look after you, how good would *you* look?

It didn't occur to anyone that their valued imports were also natives—albeit to other parts of the world. But they'd had the benefit of proper breeding and selection, and therefore looked civilized. A high percentage of the imported plants you buy today at your local nursery are graduates of this selection process and come from test beds in Europe and Japan.

Then, back around the mid- to late seventies, a remarkable thing began to happen. Gardeners started waking up to the thousands of native plant species all over the country. Why this change of attitude? For one thing, we're facing water problems as never before. Not just shortages and water rationing, but increased salinity. The native plant movement is probably as significant in the history of gardening as the invention of the garden hose.

Today, virtually every state has an active native plant and/or wildflower society. National and regional gardening magazines regularly feature articles on natives. Botanic gardens and arboretums all over the country are displaying native plants and are recreating native plant habitats. Even garden clubs, long-time bastions of traditional gardening, are now including programs and speakers on natives, and many have added native plant conservation to their bylaws.

If you want to have a successful and beautiful garden, you've got to use native plants. Otherwise, you'll continue to lose shade trees, lawns, shrubs, and other mainstays of your landscape. And, the gardens in your area won't have enough bio-diversity to stave off epidemics of plant diseases or insect invasions that chemical warfare cannot solve.

In a garden that imitates the principles of nature, there is balance and beauty; most problems take care of themselves. So, stop fighting Mother Nature, and let her do your gardening for you. She's the best gardener of all.

All or Nothing?

My sister-in-law shocked me one day. She told me that she really liked native plants but wasn't going to use them in her landscape. She simply didn't want to give up all those other plants she also loved.

That really brought me up short. When and how had I given her the idea that using natives was an all-or-nothing proposition? And, how many others had I inadvertently infected with that silly notion? It made me realize that when a person has access to the public via the printed page or the airwaves, there's no telling how much mischief can be created.

Well, I immediately started mentally rummaging through the articles and books I'd written, the talks I'd given before garden clubs and environmental groups, and even conversations—casual and business—I'd had with clients and friends. And, honestly, nowhere, no how, no way, to the best of my recollection, had I ever stated that if you used natives you had to get rid of all of your other beloved plants. That just wouldn't make sense in landscapes, like hers, where many non-native, but well-adapted, plants are already well established.

My philosophy has always been to use what works. My own landscape is only 50 percent native, the rest is composed of naturalized plants and a few cultivars of more exotic origin. Some of the non-natives were here when I moved in. I added a few others myself to see how they'd do. (My garden is, to some degree, a test lab; there is no telling what you're likely to find there from one month to the next.)

But, at the same time, I *do* think that there are instances where going 100 percent native makes a lot of sense. For example: When you build a home on a beautiful, untouched lot, the only sensible thing to do is to preserve that beauty. Why add a bunch of incongruous plants that are on sale at the local nursery and mess up a gorgeous landscape that is already installed and taking care of itself very nicely, thank you? Also, if you build on abandoned farmland that is overrun with weeds and alien invaders (plants, not Martians), getting rid of that mess and recreating the natural landscape that might have been there originally can be a very exciting and rewarding experience.

You'll enjoy finding plant treasures to add to your landscape or discovering those that magically arrive on their own. The wildlife and the marvelous complexity of nature that appears is a year-round treat. And, I must add, the lack of heavy-duty maintenance and the money you can save on water and fertilizer are just as important as the aesthetic pleasures you'll get.

This is a relatively new way of looking at landscaping. In the early 1900s, famed landscape architect Jens Jensen designed many city parks and residences in and around Chicago using this concept. In the 1930s, the University of Wisconsin at Madison recreated a prairie and three kinds of native Wisconsin woodlands. More than half a century later, their efforts are examples to all of us.

These totally natural habitats are possible in established urban or suburban neighborhoods, but admittedly, they're not always practical; you might have a neighbor who'd get uptight about a yard that didn't look like a clone of everyone else's on the street.

In that case, you can use natives in a more conventional design: Natives are well-suited to all sorts of gardens, even, believe it or not, formal ones. Using indigenous evergreens, I designed a very formal garden in the *Native Texas Plants* book with parterres and symmetrical plantings, just to prove it could be done. The design would not have looked out of place in front of an English country home, even though the plants were all quite different.

If you have a conventional landscape that you enjoy, think of native plants as hardy, beautiful additions to your garden. When those not-so-well-adapted trees, shrubs, and flowers die off in droughts, freezes, and floods, replace them with native plants.

The good news is, we're seeing more and more natives on the market these days. Growers are now providing a gorgeous array of carefully selected specimens, as well as some hybrids and cultivars that retain all of their native vigor. Added bonuses include longer flowering periods, stronger stems, or bigger blooms.

A minister I know once said, "When you're dogmatic, you paint yourself into an intellectual corner." I agree. Enjoy the rich diversity that native plants have to offer. But, when you have non-native plants that also do well in your area, by all means use and enjoy them, too.

When a Native Isn't

Usually, when I give a talk somewhere, I get introduced as a true "Native Texan." Until recently, I never gave that phrase much thought. After all, I was born in Texas, as were my parents and three of my four grandparents. And if that doesn't assure my nativeness, then add the fact that my birthday is March 2—Texas Independence Day!

Then one day my husband referred to himself as a "naturalized" Texan, having come here in the late 1960s from back East. That's when it struck me. "I'm naturalized, too," I said. "Biologically speaking, that is."

To qualify as a native, a plant (or animal) must have been here when Columbus landed. Often they've been here thousands of years; that's why natives are so well-suited to their environment. That's also why the only people who can claim to be "Native Texans" or "Native Iowans" or "Native Californians" are the Native Americans whose roots go back twenty thousand years or more.

The rest of us are like naturalized plants, relative Johnny-come-latelies having arrived within the last few hundred years; some are still arriving. These plants were native to environments similar to ours, so they've been able to survive nicely in the wild here. That's how you define a naturalized plant: no matter how it arrived—in a bag of cattle feed or on the bottom of some pioneer's boot—it must have strayed out into the wild and survived.

We've been, often unintentionally, sowing American soil with foreign plants right from the beginning. In 1672, John Josselyn published his book *New England's Rarities Discovered,* in which he listed twenty-two weeds, including dandelions and plantain, that had already been introduced into the New World from Europe. Today according to Missouri Botanical Garden we have approximately 2,200 in the continental United States—almost one-tenth of all our flora.

Most people have no idea which wild plants are natives and which are interlopers; some naturalized plants, however, have names that give us a good clue that they came from somewhere else: Japanese honeysuckle, Russian olive, and Norway maple. Others have very misleading names, like California privet (*Ligustrum ovalifolium*). This privet is from Asia, like all of the ligustrums we use; it just entered our country through a port in California.

Many naturalized plants have made themselves thoroughly at home here. These plants have intruded into all of the wild spaces around cities and are encroaching on our more remote wild landscapes. They often look weedy and act overly aggressive, and because most people think they're native, they give our own poor blameless native plants a bad name. If only that were their greatest sin.

There is a bottomland woods near my home that is green in the winter with naturalized Japanese honeysuckle and three kinds of naturalized ligustrum. There is simply no clue left as to what used to inhabit this bottomland woods before these foreign invaders took over and choked everything else out, except the taller trees. Were crossvine, coral honeysuckle, spiderworts, and eupatorium here? Could be; they like moist, shady places and are native to this part of Texas. And, I've read that at one time in this spot we had palmettos (*Sabal minor*), those short palms that form the basic groundcover along some parts of the Gulf Coast.

Have you ever gone up into the mountains of Colorado in the summer to admire the wildflowers? There are places there where no naturalized plants yet exist. When a road is cut or there is a landslide and the bare red earth is left raw, instead of ugly weeds the first plants to take over and heal the cut are native penstemons and other wildflowers. This used to be true everywhere in this country.

To be fair, some naturalized plants make good companion plants in a native garden; almost no one gets upset about blackberry lily (*Belamcanda chinensis*), jonquil (*Narcissus jonquilla*), or watercress (*Rorippa nasturium-aquaticum*). But most of the naturalized plants in our country are, at best, a nuisance. The nutgrass, chickweed, goosegrass, horehound, and other noxious weeds in our gardens are pests.

The sad fact is, these naturalized plants are here to stay, and some of them do great harm to our native environments. Kudzu is one of the worst. Anyone who has driven through the South has seen it lying like a smothering blanket over pines, oaks, phone lines, toolsheds . . . whatever can't get out of its path. Yet, believe it or not, there was a time, not so very long ago, when millions of kudzu seedlings were being grown annually. And the reason was simple: Government agencies were recommending it for erosion control.

Today, happily, that practice has been stopped. But other, equally harmful, intruders are still being encouraged. According to Leslie Sauer, Landscape Architect with Andropogon Associates in Philadelphia, Russian olive, Chinese tallow, and Norway maple are being grown and distributed in great numbers to wild and urban areas by those same agencies.

And only a few months ago, at the end of a talk I gave somewhere, a very nice lady came up to me and asked if I knew where she could get some kudzu.

Zeroing in on Your Own Backyard

My first bit of advice to people determined to attempt things reluctant to thrive on an unsuitable soil would be: Don't. It is much better to stick to the things that happen to like the kind of soil you have got in your garden and give other things a miss. I know this is a hard saying, cutting out a whole lot of temptations, but I am sure it is a right one. It is not good trying to force plants to adopt a way of life they don't like; they just won't have it unless you are rich enough to undertake excavations the size of a quarry.

VITA
SACKVILLE-WEST

Cenizo
Leucophyllum frutescens

Taking a
Regional View

At the risk of sounding like I work for the Texas State Chamber of Commerce, I'd like to say that one of the nicest things about living in this state is the marvelous diversity of terrains, climates, rainfalls, and soils found here.

Look at it this way: Texas is the United States in microcosm. Want rugged mountains? Or a true desert? We've got 'em. As well as seashores and subtropical swamps, prairies, and pine forests. Each specific set of conditions is host to a colorful array of native plants that thrive there—and sometimes only there.

Notice, I'm talking about regions, not states. States are artificial, man-made contrivances, and plants don't pay much attention to lines on maps. Take, for example, a plant such as crossvine, *Bignonia capreolata*. It's native along the Gulf Coast, all the way up to New Jersey and inland to Illinois—a region that extends far beyond what we normally refer to as a geographical region like the Southeast.

This is really the point. You have to know what works where you are. Sagebrush that thrives in Utah, for example, isn't going to be too happy in Bucksnort, Tennessee. (Yes, Virginia, there is such a place, and it's famous for smoked trout.) Even if it were possible—and ultimately, it really isn't—we wouldn't want Utah to look like Bucksnort. (No offense, Bucksnort.)

It's that unique sense of time and place and local character that fosters pride in an area. And, much of that uniqueness comes from the native plant life. Ideally, local plants should interact with the local architecture and create a harmonious, natural ambience.

For instance, picture a lovely Southern antebellum home complete with a two-story columned porch. Now, envision it surrounded by live oaks draped in Spanish moss, palmettos, and southern magnolias. This is a landscape that looks right at home along the Gulf Coast. But, imagine that house and landscape outside of, say, Tucson, Arizona. The scene would be so jarringly out of context in that Southwestern setting—well, it would make your teeth hurt!

In the Southwest, you'd want a lovely desert home built in the Spanish style, probably adobe, and you'd surround it with a green-trunked, yellow-flowered paloverde tree with yuccas, cacti, bursage, and pink penstemons underneath. That's a naturally lovely scene for that part of the country. If the Sons of the Pioneers rode up singing "Tumblin' Tumbleweed," you'd see nothing amiss.

Each landscape, in its proper setting, needs a minimum of water and maintenance to look its best. But, each would be an immense amount of trouble, if not impossible to accomplish, on the other's home ground. Yet I've seen any number of landscapes just as incongruous. Would you believe banana trees in Oklahoma?

We human animals persist in trying to dominate our environment, to bend it to our will, and to alter it to fit our ideas. We can succeed for a time. We can use unconscionable amounts of water keeping St. Augustine and Kentucky bluegrass lawns green, when native buffalograss would look as lush with a fraction of that water. We can truck in soils and hope to fool the plants into thinking they aren't really growing on limestone or in clay instead of in sandy loam. And, we can spend inordinate amounts of money on fertilizers, trying to maintain these interlopers.

In the end, of course, we are going to fail. The imported plants will die in droughts with which they aren't genetically able to cope. The late freezes will damage the alien trees and shrubs that haven't learned to wait out these tricks of nature.

And, guess what? The public (not you, of course) will go on out to their nurseries and buy the exact same plants, trying once again to make them live where Mother Nature never intended them to be in the first place.

You know the old adage: "If at first you don't succeed, try, try again." When it comes to gardening, however, the adage ought to read, "If at first you don't succeed, maybe Mother Nature is trying to tell you something."

Provenance Is Not a
City in Rhode Island
∽

Provenance is the Anglicized version of a Latin word that means roughly, "from whence it came." At this point, you're probably thinking, "Who cares?" Well, if you buy plants and you want them to be healthy, you should care a lot.

When we talk about the provenance of, for example, a live oak, we aren't referring to the species as a whole, *Quercus virginiana* and about six others depending on whose nomenclature you follow, we're talking about one particular live oak tree. We're talking about the one at your local nursery, the one over by the fence, the one you're thinking about buying. You may know that live oaks in general are native from the southern Atlantic coast to central Texas and Oklahoma. But that isn't the same as knowing that this particular live oak tree, with its own unique set of genes, is native right around Savannah, Georgia. In other words, its provenance is Savannah.

Why is this important to know? Well, if you don't mind my using Dallas as an example, we had a heck of a winter back in 1983–84. We were deep-freeze city. (I don't expect any sympathy from you folks in Montana and Minnesota, but believe me, for Texans, it was coooold!) Half of our live oaks popped their bark and died. That half included those trees sent here from growers in Houston and southern Louisiana. The other half—the ones that were totally undamaged—came from our neighbors in Fort Worth.

If you're getting ready to spend about $1,500 for a live oak or a maple or whatever, it sure would be nice to know that your tree had the right provenance for your brand of winters.

But provenance affects more than winter-hardiness. Drought and summer-hardiness are also important. Possum-haw (*Ilex decidua*) is a gorgeous ornamental tree that is native from Virginia to Illinois and down to the Gulf of Mexico; the female is ablaze with red berries from November through March, when the new leaves appear. There are a number of selections of possumhaw found in our local nurseries. Some have yellow berries, some orange, some have bigger berries, and so on.

But, all of these nursery clones were developed from possumhaws that are native to the Carolinas, where the rainfall averages up to thirty inches a year *more* than it does in that tree's western range. Do you think those Carolina possumhaws are going to appreciate arid summers and be in the pink of health? Not likely. They will be drought-stressed and hurt by insects and diseases. But the possumhaws whose provenance is western will not. Unlike the imported ones, *our* natives require no maintenance except for an occasional bit of cosmetic pruning. And they are equally varied and pretty.

The calendar itself can spell disaster for a plant of the wrong provenance, specifically during the first norther in the fall and in the first false flush of spring. This is because plants have two main mechanisms for figuring out when winter and spring are coming for real.

Some plants are light sensitive. As the days become shorter, they quit growing, send sap down to their roots for safekeeping, and get all battened down for winter. A red oak from hardiness Zone 7 should certainly be winter-hardy in Zone 8, right? Maybe not, because the days get shorter earlier in Zone 7. This red oak will keep growing and waiting for the short-day signal and get caught by a blue norther. It will never get a chance to have beautiful red fall color, and it might suffer severe freeze damage, even though it could endure much colder winter temperatures.

Northern-selected fruit trees get their flowers nipped in the spring for the same reason; longers days in the South fool them into thinking that spring is further along than it really is.

The other way plants try to tell the seasons is by temperature. If they expect 40°–50°F nights to give them a clue that winter is coming, they can be caught entirely by surprise in the Great Plains area.

For a plant (especially a tree) to withstand all of the vagaries that the weather might produce, it needs to be from the same latitude, from the same altitude, the same distance from the moderation of the ocean, and the same distance from the mountains that affect rainfall patterns. Also, it must have the same kind of soil porosity, with the same range of alkalinity or acidity. Otherwise, some norther or drought will damage it.

So, before you buy, make sure your plant is right for your climate. Purchase a plant whose provenance is within one hundred miles of where you live. Ask the people at your nursery. If they don't know, they should be able to find out for you.

Danger in
Your Bookstore

Beware. **Danger lurks** on the shelves of your bookstore's gardening section. No, I don't mean a heavy tome is likely to topple down on you from the top tier; I'm referring to the misinformation you're likely to pick up from perfectly nice, well-meaning, and extremely knowledgeable gardening authors.

A large number of those gardening books are marketed to the entire country; including you and me and millions of other people living between the Hudson River and California. But many of the authors of those books live in New England and New York and along the Pacific Coast. And, sometimes they forget about you and me out here in the hinterlands. They forget that what works so well for them may not work for us.

Remember that classic Steinberg poster showing the United States as seen from New York City? There's the Hudson River, and off on the horizon is California, and in the middle of the poster is this vast blank gray area—where most of the rest of us live.

What brought this to mind was recently reading a book on trees by one of America's foremost plant gurus. I have to tell you that I'm a great admirer of his work and use one of his books on a daily basis.

I just wish I could be as enthusiastic about his tree guide. This "definitive" work contains detailed entries for over 1,100 recommended trees, along with a list of 1,300 "inferior" species and varieties. Only a handful are listed as suitable for us here in Texas. There are probably only a handful suitable for where you live, too.

Bear with me for a second—I'm talking about Texas here, but the point I'm making concerns most of you, too.

The thing is, you'd never know from looking through this book which trees Texans ought to use and which ones they ought to avoid. Without any other, more localized, information as a guide, the Texas homeowner is prone to purchase and plant countless trees that do very well in New England or Northern California but are unsuitable for this state. These trees consume too much water in water-poor regions; they succumb to our heat, saline water, and differently timed freezes, and they fall prey to a wide range of diseases and insects because they become so stressed.

Conversely, this author lists among his "inferior" trees the Mexican plum, presumably because it does poorly in New England. Well, yes, I guess it does grow poorly—there. For most of Texas, however, it is magnificent. But notice, I said for *most* of Texas; you can't really recommend one tree that can be used well throughout the entire state. So, of course, you can't do it for the entire country.

Here's how some of our very best Texas trees are rated in this book:

- Carolina buckthorn: "inferior" to an "undesirable" species from Manchuria (What does our climate have to do with Manchuria?)
- White ash: "often considered a weed"
- Texas ash: "inferior"
- Pinyon pines: Of our three native pinyons, he only mentions the Mexican pinyon, and it is not recommended. Ridiculous!
- Wax myrtle: "not too dependable as a tree" (Does that mean that it freezes back in Boston?)
- Mexican olive: not even mentioned
- Texas redbud: not even mentioned

I don't mean to single out one author; this kind of thing is all too common in far too many gardening books that purport to talk to a national market. They are mostly written by those who rarely understand our special needs and conditions.

A few years ago, another popular garden book writer from the East was in Dallas on a promotional tour for her latest book. I caught her on a local call-in talk show, and the program was really an eye-opener. The callers asked her specific how-to questions, and her responses were more often than not, "Well, you'd better ask your local nursery about that." Really? Well, lady, why should we buy your book if you don't know any more about us than that?

Until recently, this type of gardening book was all that was available. This has influenced not only the Texas nursery industry, but also our landscape architects.

Notice, I said until recently. Today, publishers are waking up to the need for regionalized gardening books, books that address the unique conditions in various parts of the country and tell us, specifically, which plants do best in which regions of each state. And we're starting to hear from regional gardening authors, honest-to-goodness local experts who actually live with the plants they write about and even get their hands dirty digging in the local soils.

Good People, Good Intentions, Bad Input

Like credit card bills, they arrive with incredible regularity. I'm referring to that steady series of sincerely passionate direct mail appeals advocating the planting of trees—with, of course, the concomitant requests for donations to be used for that purpose.

The movement to plant new trees is vast and well organized. I've received stacks of newsletters from various groups, full of inspiring tales of how some small town somewhere has organized a community tree-planting effort. And it's rare to find a garden show or environmental seminar that doesn't include at least one speaker on urban and suburban reforestation. Sometimes, saplings are for sale right outside the door, discounted to encourage audiences to buy 'em and plant 'em. Some organizations will even give you a free tree if you promise to plant it and get it established. I receive many such offers in the mail.

This sounds marvelous, and at first glance we should all be glad that this movement is so aggressive and enthusiastic.

I'm all for planting more trees. And I'm delighted to see that many others are too. We need good healthy trees so that we can go on being healthy ourselves; so all that carbon dioxide being produced by cars and industry can be converted into oxygen. Senator Al Gore, in his thoughtful and disturbing book, *Earth in the Balance,* writes: "Forests represent the single most important stabilizing feature of the earth's land surface, and they cushion us from the worst effects—particularly those associated with global warming—of the environmental crisis."

What's wrong with this admittedly noble effort? Plenty.

Example: One free-tree offer I received included a list of ten saplings from which I could pick. Seven were totally unsuited to the soil and climate where I live; they would use too much water and ultimately die anyway. The other three were only marginally okay.

From time to time, at various meetings and seminars, I find myself sharing guest-speaking chores with representatives of some of these organizations. Again, young trees are offered to encourage planting. Many, if not all, of these trees are wrong for the areas where the audiences live. When I ask these speakers about this, they appear genuinely surprised by my question; apparently it had never occurred to them that it makes any difference.

What a tragedy that most of these groups are urging people to plant the *wrong* trees. Can there be a wrong tree? Isn't any tree better than no tree? No. There are two types of wrong tree: the kind that is good in the right place but ill-adapted where it is being distributed, and the kind that is short-lived and trashy no matter where you plant it. Either will take up space, water, fertilizer . . . and then in a few short years, sometimes in just a few months, waste that investment by dying and producing more methane and carbon dioxide as it rots and takes up space in a landfill.

The wrong tree makes the problem worse, not better.

Slash pines (*Pinus elliottii*), fast-growing trees that love acid soil and fifty inches of rain a year, are a disaster for alkaline clay and limestone where rainfall averages twenty-five to thirty-five inches a year. But, in the past year or two, countless slash pines have been distributed to the wrong locales by well-meaning people.

Actually, distributing even the right tree in the right place in massive quantities can be dangerous. Many of the trees you buy at nurseries have been grown from cuttings or were grown from seed gathered from the same few mother trees. They are genetically akin, and are therefore vulnerable to a mass infestation of some disease or pest.

Furthermore, just because one species of tree is native

over a wide range, doesn't mean that individual trees of that species will do well any old place within that range. Let's say you're distributing a widespread and important tree such as bur oak (*Quercus macrocarpa*); you can't have a grower gather seed from a grove in Tennessee and then send out seedlings to Vermont, North Dakota, Kansas, and Texas. True, bur oak is native to all those states, but there's very little chance that the ones from Tennessee will have the right genetic make-up to survive in those other environmentally diverse places. (See "Provenance Is Not a City in Rhode Island.")

It's also important to have a variety of trees. Every forest is composed primarily of more than one species, even when you count only the tallest canopy trees. Just west of Boulder and Fort Collins, Colorado, on the lower slopes of the Front Range of the Rocky Mountains, ponderosa pine and Douglas fir are the two dominant trees, with Douglas fir more frequent on the north-facing slopes. Cottonwoods (two kinds) forest the creek bottoms. You would not be doing anyone a favor by sending bur oaks or slash pines here.

Colorado changes drastically, however, as you go higher into the mountains. Subsidizing the planting of ponderosa pines in Boulder is admirable, but sending them to Aspen would not be; Aspen is at a much higher elevation where Douglas fir, aspen, limber pine, and lodgepole pine are the important components of the forest. Conversely, these beautiful trees would not be happy in Boulder.

In Maryland, there are many more species of trees and the forests are much richer in variety, but there are still distinct kinds of forests. The coastal pine forest is composed of loblolly pines, scrub pines, and pitch pines, growing where conditions are best for each. The hardwood forest is more complex. White oak, chestnut oak, Spanish oak, black oak, black jack oak, post oak, willow oak, three kinds of hickories, sweet gum, beech, tulip tree, red maple, and black gum dominate.

Obviously, it would be daunting, if not virtually impossible, to offer all these trees for reforestation at any one time. However, tree distributors in such rich forest areas might consider growing and offering a different, rotating selection of two or three suitable trees each year.

To successfully reforest America, we can't simply choose three species—or ten or even twenty-five—and send them any old place. The growing and the distribution should be localized. To insure survival through summer, winter, wet years, and dry years, the trees need to be propagated from trees that are natives right in the immediate vicinity.

In our park systems, as well as other public lands, such as large school yards and along highways, the smartest, easiest, and most efficient way to increase our woodlands and insure getting the best possible plants is also the most economical. The way to do this is to start a program of contour mowing. In the areas left unmown, seedlings from existing trees will quickly get established, and Mother Nature will select the healthiest. After about five years, if you want a more parklike look, you can cut down excess saplings and start up mowing again. However, to provide good habitat for wildlife, all parks should establish permanent lines of contour mowing that leave large areas untouched and wild.

Urban and suburban reforestation is not as simple as handing out free trees. But it really isn't all that tough, either. It's not only worthwhile, it is vital. Let's just do it correctly.

Be the First Person on Your Block to Have an Ecologically Sound Landscape

How can I break this to you gently? If you're an average American homeowner, your present landscape is undoubtedly an ecological disaster. It doesn't have to stay that way.

The best way for you to start having an ecologically sound landscape is to radically change your ideas about gardening, especially those that concern soil and bugs. The post-World-War-Two tradition of "rescue by chemical warfare" is now thought to be more destructive than helpful. Hundreds of garden advisers are now turning to nature to figure out ways to combat bugs and diseases and to grow healthier plants in an ecologically safe manner. After all, Mother Nature kept things going for millions of years, while we seem to have polluted our soils and water and air to an amazing extent in less than fifty. By studying and imitating nature, scientists are unearthing some interesting information and some novel approaches on how to garden.

The basis for all ecologically sound gardening is the soil. Healthy soil is not an inert substance; it is alive with millions of micro-organisms. These microscopic plants and animals make nitrogen available to higher plants. They also move air and water through the soil. All of these activities are essential for healthy plant life. Nitrogen fertilizers suppress these microbes until they become greatly reduced in number and are unable to function. Toxic pesticides, fungicides, and herbicides kill these important microbes outright.

Is your soil dead? If you are a traditional gardener who applies pre-emergents every spring and sprays every time you see an insect or a brown spot on your lawn, then your soil is probably dead. At the very least, it's in a deep coma.

It can be brought back to life. The first step is to stop spraying poisons. The second is to stop using fertilizers high in nitrogen salts. The third step is to start rebuilding your soil the organic way.

Some organic experts recommend a "shotgun" approach in which you aerate the soil, add compost, and spray liquid seaweed or fish emulsion or mixtures of these and other substances on the leaves of your plants until the soil has healed itself. Aeration and compost are the two big steps, because they will restore the microbes to the soil in abundant numbers.

There are many ways to aerate soil, and compacted soils aren't the only kind that need it. If, for example, the soil has been chemically abused for years, it is badly in need of aeration. This can be done physically by tilling, by turning the soil with a pitchfork or by a mechanical aerifier that punches deep holes in the ground.

After aerating the soil, dig in plenty of composted material. Soil with a high humus (compost) content absorbs rain water readily and holds it longer than soil denuded of humus. Clay soils naturally retain humus more easily than sandy soils through which moisture runs very fast, leaching out the nutrients and minerals.

Any organic matter that is broken down to the consistency of potting soil is perfect. This can be compost you make yourself, sacks of composted cow manure, or truckloads of "dairy compost," as one supplier delicately calls it.

Making your own compost is best. You can recycle all grass clippings, fallen leaves, and organic garbage in one compost pile, which takes from six months to a year to compost. Heavier wood and brush obtained from pruning can be used in a brush pile. Brush takes two or more years to compost, but in the meantime, it makes a home for small reptiles like anoles and numerous helpful insects like spiders. (Maybe it's because *Charlotte's Web* made an early and strong impression on me, but it really sickens me to see how thoughtlessly we kill spiders for no other reason than that they are there. Be glad they are, and protect them.)

Getting back to composting, wait until you hear what they're doing in Fredericksburg, Texas. Since the early seventies, residents have been raking their autumn leaves into piles near the curb. (No plastic bags!) The city then comes by and picks them up with a leaf-picker. The leaves are carted off to the sewage treatment plant and spread into two parallel rows that are closed off at the ends to make a narrow pond. Sludge is pumped in between the rows at intervals, and the piles are turned with a front-loader until everything has turned to compost. Residents then drive over in their pickup trucks and buy back their leaves—now as enriched compost—for $3 to $8 a cubic yard, considerably less than store-bought fertilizers.

Although this is not a money-making proposition for the city, there is a long-term advantage in cutting landfill costs. They are planning to expand the program to include grass clippings and brush. They are also planning to speed up the composting process. Relying on rainfall as they do now, the leaves take a year to compost. If watering is added to the process, the leaves could be composted by spring, in time to accommodate grass clippings which could be composted by fall. Is your community doing something like this? If not, dash off a note to your mayor.

How do you dig in compost if you only have established beds? Take your cue from nature. What does nature do each year to renew the soil? The answer is mulch. It is rare to see bare soil in nature. In woodlands or forests, the soil is protected and renewed by a mulch of dead leaves. In prairies and meadows, a thatch of grass litter does the same thing.

Traditionally, landscaped beds were proudly kept weed-free so that only bare soil showed around the plants. Surprise! It is now suspected that even weeds are ecologically preferable to exposed soil. Some experts recommend three to four inches of mulch, topped off all year. Some apply it once in the spring. I prefer to spread on one to two inches of composted manure or sludge in late spring to protect the ground in the summer. For the winter, I rake in fallen leaves which decompose in early spring, after providing a comforter all winter.

Mulches do much more than add organic matter to the soil; they also aid in temperature control. Bare soil in the summer in full sunlight can bake at 122°F. With a mulch, your plants' roots can stay a comfortable 82°–84°F.

Mulches also help retain water. The amount of evaporation of water from soil or through the leaves of plants can be immense. Estimates for West Texas and the Southwest deserts far exceed the annual rainfall averages. Stones can be an effective mulch in those xeric areas where organic mulches are not feasible because there is not enough organic material to make enough mulch for everyone.

Once your soil is in good shape, insect damage is minimal. This is a hard connection for many people to understand. But, sickly plants are more attractive to insects. It's like wolves preying on only the old or weaker members of the bison herd.

Once you stop spraying insecticides, you'll also have fewer insects that are harmful to your plants because you won't have killed their natural predators. Ladybugs, praying mantises, and, even more important, spiders gobble up thousands of aphids every day. Unfortunately, these longer-lived, more specialized insects are far more vulnerable to poison than the spider mites and aphids you are trying to get rid of.

Birds are harmed when they eat poisoned insects, and so are bats. (Yes, I love bats, too! Now you know it all.) Here in Texas, red bats and free-tailed Mexican bats are responsible for eating literally tons of mosquitoes each summer. There are actually *fewer* mosquitoes when bats eat them than there are if the bats are killed and man tries to control the mosquitoes with poisons.

In an unpoisoned, natural garden, there is a variety of insects but not too many of any one type. You'll have a good balance of bees and butterflies, ladybugs and caterpillars (which might become butterflies), pill bugs (which also make compost) and June bugs (to feed the mockingbirds), cicadas (so it *sounds* like a summer afternoon) and so on.

Another way to reduce insect damage is to plant a greater variety of plants. If, for instance, you have an entire flower bed planted in marigolds, spider mites will be attracted to the marigold feast. But, if you have only a few marigolds and thirty other kinds of perennials and annuals, no one kind of insect will be attracted.

Of course, in the process of converting your garden to an ecologically healthy one, before everything is in balance, you still might get a major aphid attack or be the convention center for a meeting of mites. If so, you can buy and release predator insects to clean up the pests for you.

It cost David Hoover, a landscape contractor in Dallas, $2,500 to spray a conventional pesticide on a fifty-three-acre business complex he maintains that was recently infested with aphids. The operation had to be done at night when there was no wind and no people to harm from drifting spray. The result was a total failure. "In some areas," he observed, "the populations actually seemed to increase after spraying."

So he released 10,000 lacewing larvae. Within two weeks, the aphids seemed to be all gone. But then, after six weeks, they were beginning to reappear. Because the lacewings live only about three weeks, Hoover released two more batches of 500 lacewing larvae each at three-week intervals to help a reproducing population get going. Today, the problem seems to be well under control, although Hoover is prepared to continue occasional releases until the system is entirely self-supporting. His cost? Just $440.

Impressed, Hoover decided to test them in his home garden. He gently placed thirty lacewing larvae on a rose bush loaded with aphids. In less than two weeks, the aphids were gone and have not returned. Can you imagine how inexpensive and easy this method would be for your home landscape? And how clear you conscience would be?

Seriously, is there anything I've mentioned so far that seems beyond your abilities? I didn't think so. And now that you've resolved to convert your garden into an ecologically sound example for all of your neighbors to ooh and ahh over, listen to this: Some folks are actually moving beyond just being ecologically sound and are imitating natural landscapes. Woodlands, prairies, and those edges where woods and grasslands meet are being successfully mimicked. This extends the habitats of our shrinking wilderness areas and park systems right into our home landscapes.

Can You
Say Xeriscape?

With all the work the Denver Water Department
has to do, you wouldn't think they'd have had time to dabble
in lexicology. A few years ago, however, they, along with
Colorado's landscape industry, coined and copyrighted a new
word: *xeriscape* (the x is pronounced like a z). The word
comes from the Greek root word *xeros,* meaning "dry."

Literally, xeriscaping means "dry landscaping," or using
plants that are drought-tolerant. It does *not* mean limiting
your gardens to the "Sun City" look, with cacti, rocks, and
painted gravel. Fact is, there are many beautiful flowering
plants that fit the xeriscape concept.

New concepts don't take hold overnight (there is still an
active Flat-Earth Society out there), and I have to report that
xeriscape is not yet a household word. You can still receive
vacant stares when you mention it to most people. And, I
don't know of anyone who has used it in a Scrabble game.
Nevertheless, it *is* becoming popular with a growing number
of professional landscapers and home gardeners alike who are
concerned with water conservation.

By the way, water shortages are not limited to deserts.
This is a problem that concerns us from New England to California. That's why water departments all over the country are
also promoting the principles of xeriscaping and are sending

out xeriscaping information along with their bills; you've probably received at least one.

Xeriscaping is really nothing more than what I call good-sense gardening. This is why natives, along with certain naturalized plants, are so ideal for xeriscaping. These plants have learned not just to survive but to thrive under the conditions in their areas, including periodic droughts and/or saline water. Transplant a native from one area of the country to another, and it won't fare as well—unless its new home resembles where it came from.

Want to save a lot of water? You probably aren't going to like this suggestion, but here goes anyway . . . Get rid of your lawn.

Sara Lowen, in her wonderful *American Heritage* article, "The Tyranny of the Lawn," points out that in some parts of the country "lawns consume as much as 60 percent of city water supplies during the summer months." I'm not a big fan of lawns, myself. I think they're basically pretty boring, not to mention terrible water-guzzlers. But, if you (or your neighbors) insist that you have a lawn in front of your home, then at least care for it with some basic water-conserving techniques.

I can't remember how many times I've driven through neighborhoods in states where there are serious water problems and seen sprinklers going full blast at noon. Much of that precious water runs off into the street and is wasted. Another large percentage of it simply evaporates under the summer sun.

Joe Henggeler, Extension Agriculture Engineer of Irrigation in Fort Stockton, Texas, has been doing numerous studies on water loss in home landscapes. He found that only 10 percent of water loss is the visible part we see running down streets and sidewalks. Forty percent can be blamed on wind drift and evaporation and another 40 percent on overwatering where water soaks in beneath the root zone. In a volunteer two-year program in Fort Stockton and Andrews, it was found that some homeowners had been overwatering by 300 percent, simply because they weren't adjusting their sprinkler systems for seasonal differences. For example, eight inches of water might be necessary for a lush garden in July, but one-half inch might be sufficient in March. Some homeowners were watering eight inches *every month!*

An important, but often overlooked, way of cutting water bills involves the proper adjustment of the timer on a sprinkler system. Most home sprinkler systems are divided into zones, with each zone designed to adequately cover its particular part of the landscape. That's why each zone varies in number of heads, head type, pressure, and flow rate. But, setting the timer for the *same* number of minutes for each zone may in fact *overwater* one zone and *underwater* another. According to Henggeler's studies, making sure each zone gets just the right amount and *no more* can save up to 40 percent of your costs.

Other tips for sensible watering:

- It should always be done in the coolest parts of the day, preferably after sundown.
- Water in two short cycles instead of one long one to reduce runoff. Better yet, use a drip irrigation or bubbler system; it's far more efficient.
- Water deeply. When the water gets down to a depth of four to six inches, the roots are encouraged to grow down deeper, where it stays moist longer.
- Aerate the soil for better water penetration.
- Use mulches, such as bark chips and straw, around trees and shrubs. They keep the roots cool and cut evaporation by as much as 70 percent.
- Check your watering or irrigation system for leaks. Even a teeny one can waste incredible amounts of water.

Of course, one of the best things you can do, in my humble opinion, is to use native plants—and that can include native grasses and groundcovers instead of conventional lawns. With natives, watering becomes an occasional thing, not a chore two or three times a week.

If you want to learn more about xeriscaping, contact your local water department or a nursery in your area that advertises and promotes native plants.

Better Things for Better Living Through . . . Organic?

When you are involved with plants and landscaping—professionally or as a layperson—it's inevitable that sooner or later someone will try to make you commit yourself on the "organic gardening versus chemicals" question. It seems to happen to me about once every three days. My knee-jerk reaction used to be, "Well, of course, I'm all for organic gardening. Who wants nasty chemicals all over the yard?"

But then it dawned on me that I was going along with that old labeling game, the way we often do in politics. Someone is labeled a liberal and a line is drawn. Someone else is labeled a conservative and we know exactly what to think about him or her. Only it's never that cut-and-dried. My friend, Charles Finsley, at the Dallas Museum of Natural History, is fond of saying that, "Nothing is always always, and nothing is never never."

So, what does it mean when someone says they're against chemicals? Well, if I recall my high school chemistry class, chemicals are nothing more than compounds made out of elements. *We* are made up of chemicals, like DNA. And many chemicals—all those containing carbon atoms—are organic!

It seems to me that what we're really talking about here is not chemicals versus organic—that's a meaningless comparison. We're talking toxic versus non-toxic.

Even that designation may be too simplistic. A lot of natural (organic) things are very toxic. You wouldn't want to eat oleander blossoms. Tapioca in its natural state is highly toxic; when we buy it as pudding mix, it's been heavily processed to make it safe. Arsenic is a deadly poison, but it's used by homeopathic physicians in a very diluted and purified form as a treatment for numerous ailments. And, of course, there's tobacco . . .

Many "organic" pesticides that are supposed to target specific garden pests but not harm the "good" critters are destructive to the larvae of butterflies or the immature form of ladybugs.

So the question is not, do we want chemicals on our lawns and in our gardens? The question is, do we want poisonous substances in our landscapes that have far-reaching and harmful effects on us and our environment?

Sad to say, much of what we buy and use today is far from safe. Read what it says on those weed killer bottles. The operative word here is "killer." Some of them warn you not to let your pets or children play on the lawn for twenty-four hours after application, or until the stuff has dried.

Victor Kimm, a deputy assistant administrator with the Environmental Protection Agency, said it pretty clearly, "Many people haven't fully appreciated the inherently toxic nature of lawn-care pesticide products." I guess not, since the EPA estimates that we're dumping over 25 million pounds of pesticides and 30 million pounds of insecticides on residential lawns and gardens each year. The National Coalition Against the Misuse of Pesticides claims the total for all uses, including industrial, commercial, and governmental settings, is 285 million pounds! And, 21 million homeowners are applying the stuff themselves without any real idea of what they are handling.

A study reported in the July, 1987 issue of the *Journal of the National Cancer Institute* indicates a possible link between an increase in childhood leukemia and parents' use of certain common garden pesticides. There is also growing concern about how some lawn chemicals interact with prescription drugs. Neither the FDA nor the EPA are currently conducting any tests on these possibly dangerous interactions.

And something else: what the heck do you do with the empty containers or the bottles that are still half full? I've got several of them in my garage, holdovers from my unenlightened days. I know I just can't dump this stuff down the drain or in the gutter, but most people do. And I can't blithely consign them to the garbage can and, ultimately, the landfill, although that is also a common practice. As far as I know, my community still has no effective program that will safely dispose of these poisons. Does yours?

Earlier this year, we got a mailing from the Water Department telling us about a ninety-eight-cent charge added to our bill. The money goes to pay for monitoring storm water runoff. When the Safe Drinking Water Act was passed a decade ago, the EPA thought our only worry was sewage. Now they know better. Runoff carrying toxic chemicals from lawns, as well as other pollutants, is a growing threat. This is one added charge I don't mind paying.

Public awareness is also changing, without which nothing else happens. The next time you think that your lawn and garden need a spritz of something to kill some insects or weeds, don't be so quick to grab the first bottle on the garden-center shelf. Think about what happens *after* the weed or the aphid is dead. Then, ask about safe alternatives. Many nurseries are now selling environmentally safe products.

And read. A number of good books are out on the subject of organic gardening: Howard Garrett's *Organic Manual,* Lantana Publishing, P.O. Box 140650, Dallas, Texas 75214, and several from Rodale Press are worth your time. Also, write to the National Coalition Against the Misuse of Pesticides at 701 E Street Southeast, Washington, DC 20003, for their pamphlet, "Safety at Home."

I guess a good rule of thumb is, don't spray your garden with anything you wouldn't want sprayed on you.

Putting It All Together

As it is, whatever the circumstances, I
have always tried to shape gardens each
as a harmony, linking people to nature,
house to landscape, the plant to its soil.

RUSSELL PAGE
*The Education
of a Gardener*

This used to be among my prayers
—a piece of land not so very large,
which would contain a garden,
and near the house a spring of
ever-flowing water, and beyond these a
bit of wood.

HORACE

Turk's Cap
Malvaviscus arboreus var. *Drummondii*

Requiem for a
Lawnmower

E veryone has heard of Murphy's Law (Whatever can go wrong will go wrong), and the Peter Principle (People rise to their level of incompetence). Now I'd like to introduce you to Sally's Axiom: The more boring the front yard, the greater the need for upkeep and maintenance.

Picture the kind of yard I'm talking about: meticulously clipped hedges, all squared off and boxy; manicured golf course-quality lawns; regimental rows of marigolds. And, of course, the obligatory cheap trashy shade tree (Norway maple, Siberian elm, or some such), probably stuck in by the builder and most likely ringed by an "inner tube" of impatiens. You see this pattern replicated in neighborhood after neighborhood, all over America.

Is this some sinister plot? How did our landscapes get like this?

Back when there was still plenty of wild land, a high-maintenance landscape—obviously the work of human hands and not nature—was a way of making people feel more in control of their lives and their environment.

After all, how would anyone know they'd just tamed the land if it didn't look markedly different. Even more important, especially in the Bible Belt where I grew up, people lived in mortal fear of what the neighbors would think of their moral character if every weed and stray branch wasn't instantly removed!

Happily, the trend is reversing. People (and gardens) are loosening up. It's okay to spend your day off having fun instead of mowing, edging, and hedging. And now, instead of wild land threatening us, it desperately needs our help to survive. Small tracts that have escaped being developed are now being preserved as parks, much as endangered animals are preserved in zoos.

Do you look upon mowing your lawn as good physical exercise . . . the equivalent of a rousing set of tennis, or a six mile jog? Or do you see it as a time for meditation, with the sound of the mower acting as a sort of mantra? Or is it expiation for your sins, along the lines of self-flagellation? No? Good, then you'll be glad to know that you can redesign your garden and hold a requiem for your lawnmower. Candles are optional.

Last summer, my husband and I bade an untearful farewell to our old muscle-powered mower. We'd been working up to this wonderful event ever since we'd moved into our present home thirteen years ago. We live on about an eighth of an acre, and our two-story house takes up about a third of that space. The land is divided into four gardens. In the front and to the right of the driveway is an oblong patch of ground roughly thirty feet by fifty feet, backing up to a courtyard wall, with the lower third sloping steeply down to the street, which long ago was a major feeder creek.

The area to the left of the driveway is very narrow and shady and stretches back alongside the house almost to the alley. The backyard is less than twenty-five feet deep between the house and the alley. The courtyard is a charming area thirty feet square with our house enclosing it on two sides and low brick walls on the other two sides.

Here is the story of how we inexpensively converted our boring, ordinary yard into a series of gardens that look pretty all year, feed numerous birds, anoles, raccoons, opossums, fireflies, and a woodhouse toad, and require no fertilizers, no insecticides, no herbicides, and almost no work at all.

When we moved in, all these areas looked essentially alike. They were all covered with St. Augustine lawn, except for a fringe of evergreen shrubs against the house or around the courtyard walls.

About mid-June of the first summer in our home, I

accepted the upkeep of the yard as my responsibility in the marriage. (Andy's was to keep a vigilant eye open for falling meteors.) To keep everything green, I was having to set out the sprinkler every night in some part of the yard, moving it around on a rotating basis, and, even harder, remembering to turn it off again. The June water bill reinforced my feeling that this was not the right way to go. Mowing those four little picky patches of lawn was also a definite bore.

I quit watering. Well, almost. Dallas is set on rich black prairie clay with a shrink-swell factor that is murderous on foundations. I wasn't so dumb that I quit watering the foundation. But I did cut back to about one soaking a month from June through September when our daytime temperatures are often over 100°F and some nights never cool below 90°F.

By September, it was very evident that many shrubs and trees were not going to survive on my regimen. I cut down to the ground everything that was too wimpy and ill-adapted. By the end of the next summer, more shrubs had eliminated themselves from my garden. Also the back lawn had been removed. It had been the most troublesome to mow, and I needed space for a flower bed.

The next fall I took a course on landscaping with native plants. I had to draw a native landscape plan for our house. I liked the front flower garden design so much that I decided to actually execute it. I left a circle of lawn in the front, but the rest of it was dug up and converted to wildflowers.

I followed my usual practice of scrounging wildflowers from vacant lots. I also ordered whatever native flowers and seeds were available from commercial sources. The ones that had been collected in my own state did infinitely better than those from out of state.

For years, the shady area to the left of my driveway had been eager to return to a groundcarpet of native violets. The lady from whom we'd bought the house apologized to me for them. She assured me that she had done the best she could by carefully poisoning them every year. By 1981, they had made a grand comeback, while the grass had just about disappeared with no help from anyone. This area was beginning to look like a woods, though it was (and still is) far from an indigenous one.

Leaves fell off the trees and remained here, a winter blanket that disappeared in early spring. I soon noticed that the clay in this part of the garden was getting soft and was pleasant to dig in. Earthworms were numerous. I started adding fallen leaves to my flower beds and refused to rake the leaves off the lawns.

The courtyard was next on my list. The tiny lawn here was particularly useless, since it sloped down precipitously, making it virtually impossible to set lawn chairs out there. So, I had the slope terraced. The lower part of the old lawn is now a patio big enough to accommodate an outdoor table and chairs. The upper part became a flower garden bordered by a knee-high, unmortared, limestone retaining wall. I tore out the last straight hedge with mixed feelings. I was delighted to see the boring line go and glad to have the extra space for hummingbird flowers, but I felt like a murderer because it was holly and perfectly healthy.

And that's the way things stayed for the better part of a decade. We lived happily with this landscape. The 350 square feet of lawn that remained was mowed every two weeks, by yours truly for awhile and then by a succession of college boys (Andy was still busily watching out for those meteors). I also spent about three days a year weeding everything else, twice in the spring and once again after frost.

Then, we had a freeze that killed the remaining lawn. I wish I could tell you that I immediately converted the rest of the front yard into a beautiful woodland flower garden. But, no, I tried to nurse that lawn back to health. I watered it daily. My water bill went up 100 dollars that summer. Just as it was back in the green of health again, my husband finally confessed: he'd always hated the grass out front anyway.

So, we dug up the last of the lawn, set our lawnmower on the curb (it was gone within the hour), and put in a lovely woodland flower garden. We selected extra large limestone flagstones and laid a gently winding limestone path from the street up to the courtyard steps and another one for the postman (which is very important so he won't step all over our flowers). The paths now wind through a profusion of Turk's cap, inland seaoats, zexmenia, spiderworts, ruellia, and other woodland flowers, all held together with a basic groundcover of horseherb.

I still spend just three days a year working in my garden. The rest of the time, we enjoy looking at it. We sit in it, we eat in it, the cats play in it, and passing joggers compliment us on it. And we can't help but feel a little smug as we watch our neighbors out mowing their lawns.

So You Think You Can Landscape a Garden, Huh?

The guidelines for designing a beautiful landscape are universal. Trees, shrubs, grasses, flowers, rocks, and water can be blended into a multitude of lovely designs with different styles and flavors. But, the specific plants you use to make your design work must be healthy, long-lived, and dependable, or your design will fall apart. To assure success, you must use plants native to your site. This is rarely done in American gardens, and that's why most of our gardens are transitional and labor-intensive.

How's this for a sweeping generality: People who are whizzes at math should not design their own gardens. I thought of this recently as I was driving down an interstate that had been landscaped by the highway department. The trees were all lined up with mathematical precision. Mother Nature would never have done that; it took an engineering mentality.

Frankly, there are people who should not even think about designing their own gardens. Good intentions alone won't cut it—just like wanting to sing an aria doesn't guarantee that you'll hit high C. The fact is, a sense of design is not learned; you're either born with it or you aren't. The best landscape designers I know are artists. And, even though their training leans heavily toward engineering, the best landscape architects I know also have artistic souls. If you're good at arranging a room so that it looks inviting, if you can make a centerpiece for the table, or decorate a cake that everyone admires, you can probably design an attractive landscape. If you also have trouble balancing your checkbook and never really got the hang of the seven-times table, then an attractive landscape design is pretty much guaranteed.

Just remember, when you step into the field of landscape design, you are working on a larger scale than usual. Don't be intimidated by the size of your canvas.

As for the rest of you—the ones who admit to having little or no artistic sense—well, you're probably *still* going to tackle a garden design, aren't you? In that case, let me give you a few pointers.

For the front landscape, make your house the focus of the overall design; your eye should immediately be attracted to the front entrance. If you live on a corner lot, you need to wrap the design around to include the side yard. It should all flow together smoothly, not be chopped up into disjointed units.

Elements such as the driveway, front walk, grass, and beds need to be in scale with the home. If the house is large and generous, your garden should be as well. Two-story houses need taller trees than ranch-style houses. Stand across the street to visualize the right proportions for your house. Look at your imaginary design from down the street as though you were arriving in a car.

In back, the focus is usually the sitting area, which can be lawn, terrace, patio, deck, gazebo, or pool. This is also the main point of view, even though the view out of the back windows is also very important. If this doesn't make sense to you, and you can't visualize a landscape design that gets you excited, go back and read the second paragraph again. Then, call in a professional designer or a talented friend to help you with this part of your plan—preferably one who needs all of his or her fingers to give you a cost estimate.

Design aside, choosing the plants, planting them, keeping them alive, and maintaining them properly is well within the abilities of *everyone*. You just have to think, trust your own observations, and not believe everything you're told. Rigid ideas about when to prune, how to plant, and what products to use are sometimes hard-won knowledge, but they are also sometimes old wives' tales. Orthodoxies also have a habit of changing every few years. I've found that patient observation of natural landscapes and good common sense are the most important qualities for successful garden design.

But, you ask, can't I get all of the information I need at my local nursery? Well, yes and no. Obviously, there are many experienced nursery people who can be founts of useful information. But, during what time of the year are you most likely to visit the nursery? In the spring and summer, when they are busiest and have taken on a gaggle of college students to help out. These helpers are often eager and willing but woefully ignorant, I'm afraid, and you're likely to go away with some bad advice. You'd be amazed at some of the misinformation I've received over the years from sincere, well-meaning part-time help.

And, unless they have a well-established demonstration garden, a nursery is not the best place to find out what your plant will eventually look like. Nursery stock is grown in an artificial environment of fake soil, heat unnatural to the season, regular fertilization and water, and overcrowding. This practice is necessary to produce beautiful plants in a short time in a small space. It's the only way plants can be grown at a price you can afford and also allows the nursery to stay in business. But, any plant from any climate and soil can be grown in this artificial environment. Just because a plant looks good at your local nursery does not mean that it will be right in your garden.

Besides, nursery plants tend to be what you'd expect in a nursery: babies. You need to know how large they will become. You wouldn't put big plants in front of little plants, would you? Of course not. But many people unknowingly do just that, not realizing that the short plant they purchased will, in a year or two, tower over the other plants behind it. A twelve-inch shrub in a one-gallon can might become a twenty-five-foot tree.

If you keep the eventual size in mind, you won't make mistakes like crowding sidewalks and driveways. And, you won't kill off sun-loving plants that wind up in the shade of another plant that you didn't realize would grow so tall.

The most important choices for your landscape are trees. They are the tallest elements in your design, and you want trees that are long-lived so that your garden will steadily improve with age. You also want them to be healthy and that means that they must be able to withstand all the extremes of hot and cold and flood and drought that your area can produce. They also have to really like the soil you have, because tree roots can cover as much as ten thousand square feet. I've known a lot of people who try, but you can't really change the geology of your property.

To meet all of these requirements, you will find that the vast majority (usually over 90 percent) of your choices will be trees native to your property. And, if you live on a hilltop, the trees in the nearest creek bottom are not native for *you*. To find out which trees are really adapted to your site, you'll need to observe the nearest forested *hilltop*.

If you don't know how to recognize one tree from another, take along a guide book. Choose a regional one, if at all possible. It is easy to get really far off track with a guide that was written for a national market. Or, take approximately one foot off the tip of a branch and carry it to a nature center or university for identification.

While you're still at the location that approximates your homesite, observe what shrubs and grasses and flowers are there, and identify them the same way. Notice which ones grow right under trees and which ones grow in full sun, which ones grow only in swales and which ones grow only on slopes, which ones seem to sucker and which ones are politely self-contained.

From an aesthetic point of view, observe which colors are especially pretty together, how the textures of certain leaves or tree trunks leap into prominence, and which forms are upright and which are spreading.

It is time to head for the nursery only when you have made up a plant list of usable species. If the plants you want are not in stock, talk to the nursery owner. If he knows he has a sure sale, he will be happy to order them from a commercial grower.

Once the design is laid out and the plants are chosen and purchased, you need to get the plants happily established in their new home. This is where common sense is of paramount importance.

Watering is difficult, like feeding a newborn baby. Plants, like babies, don't adhere to a strict schedule. When they're thirsty, they want attention *right away!* Some soils hold moisture for a long time and others dry quickly. Some plants prefer to grow roots in very moist soils that would make others rot. Some plants have leaves that droop dramatically when they are thirsty and give you only two or three days to rescue them.

Others are stoic and look fine until they suddenly turn crispy, and then it's too late.

Soak the area around the plant thoroughly right after planting. Check the soil dampness with your finger frequently for the first couple of weeks and regularly through the first summer. For trees and large shrubs, check through the second summer, too. Even during the cooler parts of the year, be sure to water if you go for a couple of months without rain.

Then, after your plants are established and growing well, all except your bedding flowers should be able to do without watering at all—unless you hit a very bad drought that goes on for several years.

Let's also remember pruning and mowing—both are vital to the good looks of a landscape, though these are aesthetic judgments. But once the basic look and timing are established, these chores can be done by anyone—even someone without an artistic soul.

I hope I haven't made the creation of a landscape sound too complicated. It really isn't all that tough. In fact, it's as easy as two plus two equals . . . uh . . .

Made for the Shade

The expression "made in the shade" connotes incredible ease and an absence of effort involved in some undertaking. Ha! Tell that to a gardener who has labored unsuccessfully for years, trying to keep some flora alive in the dark shadows of a giant tree or along the northern side of a wall.

These shade gardeners are numerous. I know, because the question I get asked most often, and usually with a note of desperation, has to do with what will survive—never mind thrive—in full or partial shade. The inquirer is usually someone who has seen countless plants succumb in a sunless location and is almost ready to assign that portion of the property to horseshoe pitching.

One of the first rules of combat is, "Know your enemy." To figure out what will work for you, we first need to talk about the three different types of shade we encounter.

Plants that thrive in dappled or partial shade might dwindle and die in the absolute shade found on the north side of a two-story building. No flower I am aware of can do well in that situation.

Total shade can be found under a low-growing, very dense evergreen such as a magnolia, where the sun never reaches. Don't waste your time here. In nature, all you'll find is a mulch of dry leaves. In your home landscape, leaves are quite acceptable. Or, you can use a mulch of pine needles, pecan hulls, or pea gravel.

There is a special kind of shade for those of you who live in the Deep South and have the joys and tribulations of gardening with live oaks, which hold their leaves for fifty-one weeks of the year. Pruning the tree up high and thinning out the interior branches helps, but the light level will still be very low, especially if you're also receiving shade from a house or building. That space doesn't have to be wasted, however; put in a deck or a patio. Use flagstone or brick set in sand so that water and air can reach the tree roots.

Dappled shade is what you typically find in a deciduous forest or woodland. There is sun all day long, but it is filtered by leaves and reaches the ground only in shifting patches.

If you have a fairly large area, at least fifteen feet by twenty feet, you can combine understory trees and ground-covers to create a miniature woodland that requires maintenance only once a year and attracts nesting pairs of birds.

In very early spring, you find the pink and white flowers of small understory trees such as redbud, amelanchier, or various kinds of native hawthorns. Wild violets and other woodland flowers also come out at this time and carpet forest floors.

After the trees have leafed out, the beauty of a woodland comes mostly from the many shades and textures of green. It is important to have understory trees and shrubs and knee-high groundcovers to give enough interest in heights. Combine plants that have large leaves with those that have very small leaves, shiny leaves with finely cut leaves like those found on ferns or meadow rue, or leaves with white undersides and leaves with red stems. Choose plants that will have clusters or different sizes of ripening fruits.

Small evergreen trees or large shrubs are important for winter beauty and for privacy screening. Using evergreens that are native to your area, as opposed to those from Japan or northern Europe, usually has many advantages. The biggest bonus is never having to water them. They will be much healthier and never succumb to a freak freeze. And there will be an added advantage—better bird watching.

If a flower garden, not an easy-care woodland, is your heart's desire in a spot of dappled shade, there are a number of flowers that bloom well in bright dappled shade all day. Your flower garden will not be as dense and colorful as an

English perennial border, but you can have an enjoyable rhythm of delicate textures and scattered color.

For spring, choose columbines or a local woodland phlox. The red or yellow columbines are better than the Colorado blue ones and much better than the McKana hybrids if you live where summers are hot. The phlox are usually lavender, with some pink, some blue, and some white.

For summer, choose Turk's cap and scarlet sage, both red, if you live in the Deep South. Far north, or up in the mountains where summers are cool, this is the main blooming season and there are lots of choices. Cimicifuga, swertias, or other white woodland species can give dramatic accents.

Fall brings cardinal flowers, asters, and lots of yellow daisies that consent to struggle in dim light.

Partial shade is usually a little sunnier than dappled shade. It is defined as full sun for part of the day and full or dappled shade for the rest of the day. If you're getting full sun in the morning, use the same plants you'd use for dappled shade, and you'll find that they will grow a little more densely and bloom more profusely.

However, if you're getting full sun in the afternoon, when temperatures are at their peak and the direct sun lasts four to five hours, you have a choice of a number of flowers and small trees that can tolerate both full sun and partial shade. They might bloom a little less showily than in full sun, but the bloom time is extended and less water is needed to maintain their fresh appearance.

Viburnums give flowers in May and colored foliage in the fall. American beautyberry, coralberry, and snowberry are shrubs that have purple or white berries in the fall and often into winter. For perennials, several of the following are probably native to your area or will adapt to a flower bed: black-eyed Susan, purple coneflower, bergamot, ruellia, spiderwort, veronica, and coreopsis.

Finding our own native understory trees and shrubs in nurseries is harder than finding Asian ones. Locating native flowers is much more difficult than finding begonias, caladiums, and impatiens, but the search is well worth the effort. Once you have experienced a shady native garden, rich in a variety of colors and textures, different at every season, fragrant with sweet and spicy scents, and alive with songbirds and butterflies, the contemporary American garden consisting of only one to three species seems incredibly boring.

How to Keep
from Killing
Your Wooded Lot

When Ed and Gigi saw the wooded lot, it was love at first sight. They bought the property and immediately began to plan their dream-home. They didn't know that within the year, much of the natural beauty of their lot would disappear.

There was a delightful cluster of small trees in front that created a feeling of woodland right where the front door would be. These small trees were actually large by nursery standards; the trunks were four to eight inches in diameter. Best of all, in the back were three majestic, two-hundred-year-old post oaks. These oaks would be the centerpiece of their backyard landscape, which included a creek on the rear property line.

Ed and Gigi noticed that the entire development that they were moving into, although brand new, still retained many mature trees. Clearly this was an enlightened developer; he had made a sincere effort to preserve the natural beauty of the land. Like many developers today, he seemed sensitive to conservation, if only for a dollar-and-cents reason; this developer realized that trees are an asset to a property, increasing both its visual and sales value.

We still run across builders today who bulldoze every trace of vegetation, level the terrain in all directions, and then magnanimously stick a few five-gallon trash trees in the front yard. But, these developers are a dying breed.

Ed and Gigi bought their lot in late spring. By November their house was built and they moved in, amid a swirl of autumn leaves. Thanks to the developer, the venerable oaks out back were preserved in a cradle of railroad ties that formed a series of terraces down the steep bank to the creek. The mini-woods in front had been attractively landscaped with shrubs, and sod had been laid. All seemed well.

When spring arrived, the three large oaks remained virtually bare. One was clearly dead, one was covered with white mildew and very likely dead, and the third oak was struggling to survive.

Was some virulent disease doing the damage?

The problem is a common one, simply a case of good intentions gone awry. The developer was unwittingly doing a lot of things wrong.

First mistake: The soil was piled up around the base of the tree trunks. This excess soil held moisture against the trunks, instead of allowing it to seep down to the roots. Mildew developed and began creeping upward, rotting the bark. Even worse, this extra soil was suffocating the trees. Most trees breathe through roots that are close to the surface, where oxygen is present in the soil. A tree's trunk should flare out slightly at ground level. If no flare is visible, soil has been piled up too high; even three extra inches of dirt can seriously harm a tree. In Ed and Gigi's lot, the trees were buried under twelve to eighteen inches of dirt.

Second mistake: Workers inadvertently hacked away at the trunks, usually by running into them with bulldozers and by piling lumber, bricks, and trash up against them. Patches of bare, exposed wood were the result, which interrupted the natural flow of sap—the tree's bloodstream. When this happens, the branches overhead die. If a tree has bark missing on more than one side, it is almost surely doomed. The surviving tree, at this writing, is hanging on only because it had the least amount of damage inflicted on its bark.

Third mistake: More than one-half the roots had been chopped off to make room for the house, the concrete-slab patio, and the railroad-tie terracing. A tree's roots extend out one and one-half times as far as the branches overhead. Destruction of the roots results in a corresponding die-back of the branches.

Ed and Gigi's loss could easily have been avoided if they (and their builder) had been aware of these facts. But, knowing the facts is not always enough.

A few years back my friend, Ron, lived through a landscaping nightmare. He had purchased a lushly wooded lot and planned to build his home there. Ron is an architect, and he knows how to preserve trees. Still, he couldn't have foreseen what eventually happened.

The trouble began because another home was being built on the adjoining lot. One day, Ron discovered that the neighbor's bulldozer had run amuck on his property and destroyed a large percentage of his mature trees. Of course, Ron collected damages, but let's face it, no amount of money can replace a thirty-year-old woods. (Not in less than thirty years, that is.)

But, the horror story did not end there. When it came time for Ron to build his own house, he gave specific instructions to his bulldozer operator. He marked off the trees that were to be saved with orange plastic ribbon and even took time off from work to stand around and supervise. Trouble was, the bulldozer operator got back from lunch before Ron did. In less than fifteen minutes, six perfectly healthy, mature trees had been leveled. (To paraphrase P. J. O'Rourke, giving a bulldozer to some guys is like giving liquor and car keys to teenaged boys.)

Ron's home was to have been surrounded by woods. He wanted no lawn to mow, no groundcover to weed, and nothing to water. Mother Nature had already provided American elms, cedar elms, bois d'arcs, and junipers in abundance. Underneath were numerous understory trees, shrubs, and groundcovers—many of them evergreen. This natural wooded landscape, besides being beautiful, would have provided privacy, shade, erosion control, noise-buffering for the nearby highway, and wonderful birdwatching.

Do you think these two stories are isolated incidents? If only that were true. These things happen all too often on individual lots, as well as on large tract developments. Here are some steps you can take to protect the existing trees on your land: Assess all of the trees on your property. There are many good tree-identification books out on the market today, so stop by your local library or bookstore. If you feel incapable of identifying all of the trees yourself, ask a competent landscaper or arborist to visit your property for a consultation. But, take care—don't get caught up in your consultant's personal prejudices. People often have very strong likes and dislikes of trees for very strange reasons. Don't accept at face value any-one's assessment of a tree as "trashy." Ask them why they feel that way. Get all the facts. And, remember that a tree you would never buy is often absolutely invaluable to your land-scape if the tree is the right size and in the right place. I per-sonally dislike hackberries, but I would weep if I lost the huge one that shades half of my house!

Pay special attention to the smaller understory trees: viburnum, redbud, hawthorn, hollies, and so on. You'll prob-ably find an abundance of them on your property. These trees are crucial to the maintenance of a true woodland look, and they provide gorgeous spring and fall color. They are also very important as nesting and feeding locales for wildlife. These understory trees, however, are usually cleared away, even by developers who make an effort to save the big stuff.

Thicket shrubs such as roughleaf dogwood or its relatives and smooth sumac should also be saved; they are useful for privacy, rounding out corners, and providing cover for birds.

The list will vary, depending on where you live, but you're also sure to find a treasury of native groundcovers and wildflowers: Virginia creeper, coralberry, coral honeysuckle, crossvine, wild asters, frostweed, violets, wild orchids, and fragrant phlox are the most frequent ones in my area. Have fun finding them, but watch out for and remove poison ivy and greenbriar.

Plan where your house and driveway will go *only after* you've identified your trees and have selected the ones you most want to save. A good architect can be very clever in think-ing of ways to keep all of your trees and have your house, too.

Wherever possible, barricade the trees out as far as their driplines. *Dripline* is the term used to describe the area on the ground directly beneath the furthest reach of the branches. This is usually where the roots are most active. Cutting the roots, burying them, or dumping building wastes such as ce-ment or leftover paint on them is severely harmful.

Use snow fencing or build barriers of scrap lumber and tie bright Day-Glo plastic ribbon prominently on the barriers. This will not only help protect the trees, but it will keep the valuable understory and groundcovers intact. Sound expen-sive? Price a few large trees and you'll find that protecting what you've got is really the most economical option.

Arrange to be on the property *whenever* the bulldozer is in operation. Don't trust verbal or written instructions. (Take short lunches!)

Oversee the grading; don't let soil get piled up on the roots, and don't let poor drainage areas develop. Standing water can suffocate a tree even more quickly than extra soil. Following the natural lines of drainage is the best choice. Also, check neighboring lots to see how they might be channeling water your way.

Make an agreement with your builder that he or she will compensate you at a fixed amount for any injured tree. Make sure your builder knows that dumping building materials on roots is just as damaging as scraping the trunk and breaking branches. Cement waste, in particular, is caustic and poisonous to trees.

After your house is finished and the workmen are gone, remove protective barriers. This is also the time to have your trees pruned. Choose someone for the job carefully. A good tree pruner is an artist who sees a tree as a sculpture; he or she would *never* cut off the end of a branch. Good pruning cleans out the middle of the tree and cuts branches off nearly flush with the main branch or trunk.

If you have a natural, wooded property, you are indeed fortunate. Protect it. Care for it. It will pay you back with great beauty and enjoyment for many decades.

Don't Let Your Wildflowers Run Wild

Wildflowers look so gorgeous growing along our roadsides that many people are fooled into thinking that they can grow wildflowers successfully—and effortlessly—on their own properties. When they try, they learn that growing wildflowers and native grasses from scratch is often unexpectedly hard work.

Sometimes hundreds of dollars of seed and a lot of physical effort result in a waist-high weedpatch. And, if you're one of those people who think wildflowers and weeds are synonymous, let's get that straightened out right now: Wildflowers have big, showy blossoms. Weeds have tiny, scattered blossoms almost hidden by large coarse leaves. Weeds usually grow three times as tall and as fast as self-respecting wildflowers. Finally, wildflowers are beautiful; weeds are not.

A weedpatch is exactly what some of my clients in Kerrville, Texas, wound up with. They wanted a low-maintenance, naturally beautiful Hill Country landscape in their front yard. They envisioned native shrubs and trees close to the house and along a fence, and a buffalograss meadow, thick with wildflowers, stretching out to the road.

Their lot was situated between two other homes, each one having a beautiful wildflower meadow. Naturally, they thought having their own meadow would be easy.

In the fall, they hydromulched with buffalograss and a

wildflower-seed mix. The results the following spring were definitely not spectacular. So, they immediately planted more wildflower seed. They repeated the process the next fall, and still again the next fall. After three and one-half years, they were thoroughly discouraged. The front yard was full of weeds.

Of the pounds and pounds of wildflower seed they had sown, only five individual flowers could be found that were of the species that had been deliberately planted. And, a fair stand of sun-loving buffalograss was being shaded out by tall weeds.

What went wrong?

First, they made the mistake of having the land bulldozed and reshaped. This only stirred up a lot of dormant weed seeds—junk stuff, trash. They would have done better working with the natural contours of the land. Because this land was a native meadow when they bought it, all they really needed was regular maintenance, which would have included cutting after the first frost.

Once the land was disturbed and they *had* to reseed, they compounded their first mistake by using an inappropriate seed mix. They chose one containing a number of wildflowers that were not at all suited to their region of the state. This is not an uncommon problem with many commercial mixes. Remember, a native plant is not native everywhere. They could have collected seed from their neighbors' wildflowers and planted them. Or, they could have purchased *specific* wildflower seeds, once they'd determined which wildflowers were indigenous to their area.

Finally, they didn't weed. They were trying for easy, remember? Well, there's no getting around it: You have to get out there and pull those weeds. And, you have to do it regularly for the first two years to allow the wildflowers to get established.

The trick is to eliminate the weeds and *not* the wildflower rosettes. (Two books on how to recognize rosettes are listed in the next chapter called "Transplanting Made Easy.") In my client's case, a simple examination of their neighbor's meadows was necessary. All of the wildflowers they eventually ended up with came from right next door.

Weeding doesn't have to be total misery. Put on a comfortable sunhat, take a jug of iced tea and a portable radio outside with you, and just imagine that some wonderful benefactor is going to give you a thousand dollars for every weed you yank.

Transplanting Made Easy

Some people think that gardening is just a warm weather activity; nothing could be further from the truth. For instance, in most parts of the country, the best times of the year for transplanting are late fall and early winter. The reason is simple: A plant that is dug out of the ground loses 80 percent or more of its root system. It needs all of the time available to grow new roots before it must face the stress of flowering, fruiting, leafing out, before it has to contend with summer heat and drought.

Most people don't realize how extensive root systems are. A ten-foot-tall oak tree with a trunk three to four inches in diameter and branches ten feet wide has a dense root network extending fifteen to thirty feet across. But, after the tree is dug up, its root ball will typically be only two to three feet in diameter. That's an enormous loss and a great shock to the tree.

That's why you should pamper a transplant with frequent watering for the first two to five years. The larger the tree, the higher the percentage of root loss may be. This means that a large tree needs more years to regrow its root system than a small tree. Until the original roots are replaced, the tree will not put on new growth. A tree with a one-inch trunk often outgrows a four-inch tree within five years of each being transplanted.

Flowers and grasses are much easier to transplant. Because they are smaller, they can usually regenerate their roots in one growing season. The optimum time to transplant anything is on a misty or drizzling day in autumn. In high humidity, the tiny hair roots cannot possibly dry out and be damaged, and your plant can start transporting moisture and growing new roots almost immediately.

Speed is also important. The faster you can get the plant back into the ground, the better it will fare.

Water the plant thoroughly after transplanting. This not only insures that plenty of moisture is available, but is also the gentlest way to melt the soil around the roots again so that no air pockets remain; air pockets allow air to dry out the roots.

Choosing Plants to Transplant

First, make sure that the plants you covet have a good chance of thriving in their new location. Choose plants from a site close to where you live and from an environment that matches or closely resembles the spot in your garden where they will go. Something from a rocky, dry area is not likely to grow well in moist garden loam.

Second—and it probably goes without saying—never dig up plants on public lands. If the plant you want is on private property, make sure that you have permission from the landowner to dig it up. This is no joke—plant rustling can land you in jail!

Third, don't be greedy. Choose a plant that is young and small enough so that you can get enough of its root system to give it a high chance of survival. I've learned from sad experience that when I move a nice big plant, a medium-sized one, and a small one, it's the small one that grows fastest and blooms first; the big one rarely survives.

Flowers and Grasses

Although flowers and grasses are easy to transplant, there are basic rules to follow.

Flowers, including annuals, biennials, or perennials, can all be transplanted in the fall, but *only* in their rosette state. A *rosette* is a sunburst of leaves that hugs the ground. The smaller the rosette, the better its rate of success. Rosettes are hard to identify, so plan to identify the plants when they are in bloom, and mark the stems with plastic flagging tape. In fall, you can easily spot the tape fluttering from dead, brown stems.

If the plant is an annual, (it goes from seed to flower and dies in one year) or a biennial that blooms the second year and dies, you will have better luck if you collect and plant seed rather than transplant. If you *do* transplant, both WildSeed's seed catalog or the book *Parks' Success with Seeds* have photos of rosettes that will help you to identify the plants you want.

Perennials are much easier. A new rosette should form at the base of the dead stalks. Do not dig until the rosette has formed. Usually, a plant marked like this will be too big to move in its entirety with any degree of success. Either use it as your guide for finding smaller rosettes of the same kind, or if a cluster of rosettes has formed around the stalk, dig out a small rosette on the edge. The new, vigorous growth is always on the outside edges.

The most desirable grasses are perennials and they can be treated just like perennial flowers. They do not, however, have rosettes. The leaves turn brown and the plant goes dormant in the winter. Dig a small portion from the edge of the mother plant. Remember to dig both outward and deeply to get plenty of roots. Use surrounding soil to fill in the hole around the exposed roots of the mother plant so it will not suffer any permanent damage.

Trees and Shrubs

Choose a well-shaped tree that is far from competing trees and roots. If the trunk is one to eight inches in caliper (the diameter at chest level), you will have the best rate of success. For each inch of trunk diameter, you need to allow for nine to ten inches of root ball diameter. Plan ahead and be aware of how many strong friends you can count on. A tree that is three to four inches in caliper must have a root ball of at least thirty to forty inches in diameter. A root ball that size requires three average-sized men (or two hunks) to lift it out of the ground.

Make sure that the tree is in digable soil. Sandy soil is difficult, because the root ball falls apart; be prepared to use plenty of burlap and wire. Rocky soil is fine for a one-inch caliper tree, unless the soil is too rocky to dig. Tight clay soil works best.

But, before you dig up that tree, go back and prepare its new home—the *receiving hole*. Make it shallow and very wide, and keep the sides of the hole rough, not hard-packed and smooth. Many plant people believe that hard-packed sides tend to trap the roots, as if they were in a pot, and prevent them from spreading out. Save the dirt for backfilling later. Fill the hole with water to make sure it will drain quickly; you should be able to see the water level sinking as you watch.

Only after you are sure that the receiving hole is ready should you dig up the tree. If the soil is too dry, the root ball will fall apart; come back a few days after a rain, or, if possible, water your tree deeply around the tree base and allow three days for the soil to dry to the right consistency of tacky-moist. If the ground is too wet, the root ball will also fall apart. (That's right, it's not as simple as you may have thought; now you know why nursery trees cost so much!)

Measure the width of the root ball and, with a clean, sharpened shovel, dig down around the perimeter, cutting cleanly through the roots. End at a point eighteen to twenty-seven inches underneath the trunk; that's where you can locate the tap root (if there is one). The finished root ball should be cone-shaped.

To hold the root ball firmly and disturb it as little as possible, wrap it with burlap and wire. If the tree is only one inch in diameter, burlap and string is all you will need. Do not use synthetic burlap, because it doesn't biodegrade and the roots won't be able to get out.

Once the root ball is firmly bound, make a sling or cradle to lift it out of the hole. Never lift the root ball out by the trunk. The weight of the soil is enough to cause tearing of the roots. From the sling, gently place the tree on a dolly or in a wheelbarrow. Cushion the trunk with burlap or old rags to prevent rubbing against metal or anything else that might injure the bark.

Place the tree in the receiving hole, making sure that it is neither set in too high nor too low. Its original soil level should be exactly even with the new soil level. Otherwise, the roots will be either too far underground to breathe properly and the tree could literally suffocate or too exposed and will dry out. If you dug the receiving hole too deep, raise the level with original soil and tamp it firmly at the bottom of the hole. If the bottom of the hole is not packed hard, it could sink and your tree could sink with it. Even an inch or two can make a significant difference.

Backfill with the original soil. Don't fill in with compost or peat moss, thinking that you are doing the tree a favor. Those lighter fills create a potplant effect, and the roots will circle in this easier-to-grow-in medium, never venturing out into clay or rocky soil. Your tree's roots need to adjust right away to the real world.

To get extra nutrients to the roots right after transplanting, top dress with compost and slow-release organic fertilizers. Natural root stimulators are also helpful.

Correct watering is probably the most important aspect of getting your tree established. Many botanists believe that the air and water balance in the soil are the single most crucial factors in the health and growth of trees. Roots grow only as deep as the air circulates in the soil. In tight clay soils, six inches is sometimes as deep as roots can go, though twelve inches and eighteen inches are more common. In sandy soils, roots typically grow deep until they hit a clay layer. The standard talk of forty-foot-deep roots is "bunkum," according to some experts I've consulted. Such rumors got started, they say, by scientists walking through cuts and stream banks, seeing roots at the bottom of the cuts. Along a forty-foot bank, you might see tree roots all the way to the bottom; that's because aeration is good along the sides of the bank.

Everyone knows that underwatering is bad because it causes roots to dry out. Overwatering is equally damaging because it drives air out of the soil. The best way to water a tree is to let a hose drip on the base slowly. Overnight is great. Let the top inch of soil dry out, and then repeat the slow soaking. Do this for the first two summers after your tree has been transplanted.

Forget These Old Ideas

For years, the common wisdom in transplanting included a lot of practices we now know to be either useless or harmful.

Do not stake, except in dire circumstances where there are excessive winds and loose soil. *Do not* prune out one-third of the tree—the more leaves you have making food (photosynthesizing) for re-growing roots, the better. *Do not* wrap the trunk; it traps moisture and invites insect damage. And, finally, *do not* plant periwinkles or impatiens around the base of the tree; you'll tend to overwater the tree. A top-dressing of mulch around the trunk is perfect.

The Biggest No-No

Do not use a weed-whacker near the trunk, as it can damage the bark and girdle the tree. This common mistake accounts for more tree deaths than anything else.

How to Transplant Post Oaks

I mention this specific tree because it's the one tree that most people are afraid to transplant. I'm told by Sandy Rose, a north Texas arborist and an expert on moving post oaks, that the only tricky part is choosing the right tree to dig. Select a young, vigorous tree four to seven inches in caliper that is on the edge of the woods, far enough from other post oaks. This guarantees that it won't be a sucker.

Yaupon Holly
Ilex vomitoria

A Yaupon Holly
Is Not a Lollypop!

If you think that this statement is a little obvious, you haven't been paying a lot of attention to landscapes. Give me a dollar for every yaupon (*Ilex vomitoria*) that's been pruned into a little "French poodle" or "lollypop" shape, and I could retire in semiluxury tomorrow.

Okay, I admit that this is all very subjective. There are perfectly nice people who give to charities, call their mothers every Sunday, and wouldn't consider using naughty words— who really like topiary (that's what they call it when shrubs and trees are pruned into rabbits and elephants and all sorts of geometric shapes). They even pay good money for someone to come out regularly to inflict this questionable art on their innocent plants.

But, I also know that lots of people who have "lollypops" in their yards never intended to. "Oh, it's just something that the landscape maintenance people do," they tell me. I guess they think that once a yaupon has been clipped in that fashion, they have to live with it forever.

Personally, I think that this multitrunked evergreen is pretty enough to stand on its own merits, especially the females, which display red berries all winter. You may not have yaupons in your area, but I'm sure that you have local evergreens that get this same treatment.

The yaupon has the potential to grow twenty-five feet tall and thirty feet wide, but this process can take more than fifty years. Because it's a slow grower, most designers plan on its occupying an area about fifteen feet by fifteen feet. At that size, it fits nicely against the front of the house, especially in the stretch of bare wall so often found between the living room and the bedroom windows. It perfectly rounds off the front corners, even when you have a one-story home. It also fits nicely into those small, dark side-gardens that must look good all year because they are seen from the master bedroom or the dining room.

But, in all of these instances, it is the natural spreading grace of the yaupon holly tree that makes it work visually. A landscape is supposed to have flow and harmony. A "lollypop" stops the flow; it is a staccato note that disrupts the rhythm.

If you've got a "lollypop" in your yard, and you think I'm full of beans, that's okay. Just turn to the next chapter—assuming, of course, that we're still friends—while I proceed to tell the rest of the readers how they can prune their yaupon holly trees correctly and get them back on the right track.

Sally's Sure-Fire Yaupon Restoration Plan:

1. You'll need two pruners: a long-handled pair about two feet long, and a smaller one-handed pair, about nine inches long.
2. Now, check the trunks. If two are growing into each other and rubbing off bark (providing an opening for infection), keep the trunk that is growing outward, removing the trunk that is growing inward. Cut it back to ground level. Check the aesthetic quality of the trunks that are left. Be very cautious about taking out trunks that are not potential problems. Have someone pull the trunk in question as far out of the way as possible, so you can see what the tree would look like without it. If you are still in doubt, leave it. You can always remove it later, but you can't glue it back on.
3. Now, start cutting off all of the branches that grow in toward the center of the tree. Cut every one of them off at the collar—that's the slight thickening of the branch where it joins a larger branch or trunk. The

idea here is to give the tree a nice, airy, open feel in the middle.

4. If the branches have been cut back so many times that the branching looks like a starburst of minibranches (a very ugly look), cut back to the first long, undamaged branch that points outward.

5. Do not cut off the end of a branch for at least five years; this allows the branches to grow long enough to give your yaupon a tree structure. After five years, if your tree is as large as you want, you can begin cutting off end branches—but *always* cut them off at a collar. Do not just snip off an end.

Yaupons can be safely pruned at any time of year, but I am always cautious of pruning in November; I don't like to stimulate tender new growth just before the first vicious norther.

And, I never paint the cuts. They gray over very quickly, and I've never had one get diseased.

Your yaupon is probably drawing a sigh of relief just knowing you are reading this and getting ready to end its embarrassment. You'll be amazed and pleased at how much better it will look instantly. And after about a month of new growth, it will look even better.

Post Oak
Quercus stellata

Leave Those Leaves

I'm going to let you in on a fabulous product for your lawn and garden. It hasn't been advertised anywhere, and you can't buy it in any nursery or hardware store. It covers your yard all winter and slowly decomposes, so that, by spring, you'll have a marvelous all-natural composted mulch.

But, that's not all! This stuff not only feeds and renews your soil, it also helps the spring rains soak into the soil better. Then—and you're not going to believe this—it actually helps retain moisture in the soil during the hot summer months.

I can see you reaching for your wallets already. "Where is this miracle product?" you're asking. "Where can we buy it?"

Well, you can't buy it. It's free, and every fall you'll find gobs of the stuff lying out there in your yard. That's right—leaves. The ones you rake and bag up in sturdy, nonbiodegradable plastic, and then have hauled off to the city landfill where, generations from now, archeologists will view the results of your weekend's toil.

We've got to stop thinking of those fallen leaves as trash. Leaves are Mother Nature's way of protecting the roots of plants from winter freezes. Fallen leaves are also nature's fertilizer.

In my yard, the leaves lie where they fall until after the first frost, when my perennial garden turns into a tangle of brown stalks. Then, I cut down the stalks to about four inches them in lightly and gently. I don't want to pack them down; I want lots of air to get trapped in with the leaves. This air remains warmer than the outside temperature, not unlike the way air trapped under a down comforter keeps us cozy. Loose leaves also allow enough light and air to reach the soil so that perennials that maintain rosettes of green leaves all winter are happy, too.

I rake leaves into the beds of my woodland area as well, and I didn't mind having a fair number on the lawn.

Now, you may not want to have your lawn covered with leaves. Or, it may be fine with you, but your neighbors would have a fit. (Although, have you noticed? There really does seem to be less of a clean-lawn fetish abroad in the land these days.) Okay, so rake those leaves up and haul them to a compost pile in your backyard.

After they've composted, spread them back on the lawn or use them in flower beds or vegetable gardens. You'll find that this works just as well as your store-bought products and is environmentally much more attractive.

When I had a lawn, I never used lawn fertilizers. A neighbor had a company come out regular as clockwork to treat her yard. Personally, I never saw any difference between our lawns. But, I have noticed that several fine trees of hers that used to shade our yard have died.

I have plenty of large deciduous trees, so there's never a leaf shortage around my house. You may not be so lucky. In that case, my advice is to steal some. Well, not actually steal, but do go out and cruise your neighborhood. When you see plastic sacks of leaves set on the curb or in the alley, do a good deed. Put them on your own lawn and save the city some work.

A Native for Every Niche

All things have their place, knew we
how to place them.

GEORGE HERBERT

Nature's laws affirm instead of prohibit.
If you violate her laws, you are your own
prosecutor, attorney, judge, jury, and
hangman.

LUTHER BURBANK

Desert Marigold
Baileya multiradiata

. . . And So to Bedding

If use translates into popularity, the most popular flowers in the plant kingdom—certainly the most ubiquitous—have to be bedding plants: petunias, marigolds, impatiens, periwinkles, and begonias, for example. Everybody, it seems, uses and apparently likes these petite beauties.

Landscape architects and contractors like bedding plants; it's difficult to think of an office building that doesn't have the obligatory massed array of bedding plants around the main entrance. Nursery owners like them because they are very profitable; myriads of flats are sold every time the seasons change, and whenever a cold snap kills the more popular imported varieties.

Amateur gardeners like these plants because they adapt so well to the confines of a modest suburban home lot; it takes only a few to make an attractive accent by a front door or as an edging by a walk or patio. Even gardening connoisseurs, who insist on variety and originality in their displays, use bedding plants to fill in bare spots and to help out abused areas near walkways.

It's easy to see why bedding plants are so popular. They're very well-behaved, forming neat mounds barely over a foot across and usually a little under a foot high. Many of them bloom like crazy for months on end without a break.

And, they adapt well to any rich, organically well-prepared, well-drained garden soil. And then, of course, perhaps the biggest reason of all: You don't have to be a Luther Burbank to use them; they thrive for the grayest thumbs among us.

Often these flowers are annuals, but even more often, they are perennials that are used as annuals where the winters are too cold for them or the summers too hot.

The problem is, we use them so often that we run the risk of becoming bored with them. The most beautiful piece of music will eventually put you to sleep if it's all that you hear. So, I'd like to introduce you to a few bedding plants with which you may not be familiar. Or, if you *are* familiar with them, you haven't been exposed to them enough to be jaded. Unlike most of the bedding plants you know already that come from tropical and subtropical lands, these plants are native to the southwestern United States. This means they'll save you water and money; they're all more drought-resistant than the bedding plants currently being marketed (except for portulaca and purslane). Furthermore, unlike overbred petunias and begonias, they provide important nectar for butterflies and pollen for bees.

Blackfoot daisy (*Melampodium leucanthum*) is, I fearlessly predict, going to become one of the most popular in the country—once everyone finds out about it. It's a tidy plant—well-behaved and always less than a foot tall and not much wider. Its small, narrow leaves are a soft green and are almost hidden by the masses of white daisy-like flowers. These flowers cover the neat mounded plant from early spring, through the summer, and until late fall, usually until Thanksgiving and sometimes later, depending on when you get your first hard freeze.

Blackfoot daisy is native from Mexico to Arizona to Kansas. It's a perennial, so if it doesn't freeze to death where you live, you won't have to plant it again next year. Those from Kansas will obviously have more cold-tolerance, while those from Arizona will have the most drought-tolerance. See how logical Mother Nature is?

Blackfoot daisy is not picky about its soil, as long as it's very well-drained. It will grow in poor rocky soil or sandy soil, but it is especially fond of rich garden soil that is loaded with organic matter.

Give it plenty of sun; it doesn't care for shade. This daisy will tolerate reflected heat, a very useful feature. That makes it ideal for edging a flower border next to a large paved area, such as a driveway or the deck around a swimming pool. It is also good in a pot on a sunny patio or in giant planters in front of a skyscraper (or whatever passes for one in your town). Use it where you frequently walk, such as on the way to your car, or where you most often sit outside. Not only does it always look good, but it is also delightfully scented. On really hot afternoons, it smells of strong, wild honey.

Yellow plains zinnia (*Zinnia grandiflora*) is another one of my favorites. The leaves are so narrow that they are almost threadlike, much narrower than those of the little orange-flowered Mexican *Zinnia linearis*. They are packed densely to form mats of foliage about eight inches in height that look a little like thrift (*Phlox subulata*). The flowers are about one inch in diameter, single, four-petaled, and bright yellow. The nectar is sweet and extremely popular with butterflies.

Yellow plains zinnia likes a lot of sun and blooms best when the weather is hot—May through October. Unlike most other flowers, the yellow plains zinnia doesn't look ratty as soon as it quits blooming. You can leave the blooms and watch as the petals dry to a delicate, papery texture and the yellow fades to an attractive ivory.

Yellow plains zinnia is a perennial that is native from Mexico to Kansas and Nevada. It forms new plants by the roots, but it is not invasive; it spreads somewhat slowly. I've heard that with patience, however, you can encourage it to become a first-class groundcover.

The various kinds of Tiny Tim (also called dogweed or dyssodia) are small mounds of finely textured foliage topped with tiny yellow daisies. There are several kinds scattered over the Southwest, and the foliage is more distinctive than the flowers. Some have lime-green foliage, some silver, some blue-green. *Thymophylla setifolia* is a good silver one. Like most silvery-leaved plants, it needs exceptionally good drainage and lots of sun. Some Tiny Tims are designated as annual, and some as perennial. Most are actually somewhere in between. They often live over a year, but rarely as long as three. They frequently die in the winter if the soil becomes too wet.

Golden globe (*Hymenoxys odorata*) is a showy golden bouquet of flowers, sometimes given the unappreciative name bitterweed. Ranchers tend to bestow that name on several species of hymenoxys and helenium that have foliage that tastes bitter to cattle and can make cow's milk taste like medicine to us. If you see a pasture filled with golden globe, it has not aggressively taken over the whole area and crowded out all of the other plants. The cows merely gobbled up all of the other tastier plants, and only the golden globe was left to hold the soil together. So, don't be afraid to buy this flower; it won't engulf all of the other flowers in your whole garden, I promise. Besides, it's awfully pretty.

Golden globe is an annual that is native from Kansas to California south to Mexico. It forms a one-foot ball of aromatic lime-green, finely cut foliage. The yellow daisies with large yellow centers are one to two inches in diameter and, at times, will almost completely hide the leaves. With occasional watering and snipping, it can be coaxed into blooming from early spring to a killing frost. It (like all the others in this chapter) prefers full sun and good drainage.

Desert marigold is also a yellow daisy, but it has layers and layers of petals on long slender stems, making it an excellent cut flower. Its leaves are covered with a fine silvery wool and mass closely together to form a low, fuzzy gray-green mound. The delicate stems radiate out of the mound to a height of approximately one foot. An excellent plant for the driest parts of the states, it's in bloom whenever the weather is above freezing. It usually lives from one to two years, literally blooming itself to death and dying of exhaustion. It seeds out fairly easily, and new plants are usually in bloom within three months.

Of course, this is just a sampling. There are many other natives that are ready, willing, and able to go to bed in your garden.

Cenizo—
Recognition at Last!

Homeowners in this country's desert regions (basically everyone from El Paso, west to Los Angeles and San Diego) seem to have two basic approaches to landscaping: They either fill their yards with rocks, gravel, and cacti, or they try to copy landscapes in Virginia and Connecticut, with carpets of thirsty lawns and all sorts of back-east-style annuals and perennials.

Yet, they are literally surrounded by a wealth of gorgeous (not to mention low-maintenance and water-conserving) desert plants that would introduce exciting new colors and textures to their look-alike yards.

Amazingly, it isn't only homeowners who are unaware of this marvelous and available native palette. I gave a talk in El Paso to a group composed largely of nursery owners and landscape architects. As I proceeded through the program, flashing slide after slide on the screen, people in the audience kept interrupting to ask me to repeat a plant name or simply to express surprise that these plants had been practically in their backyards all along.

Let me introduce you to just one desert plant that I'm particularly fond of, a lovely silver-leaved, lavender-flowered shrub called cenizo (*Leucophyllum frutescens*). It also goes by other common names: Texas Ranger, Texas sage, barometer bush, and Texas silverleaf. (No, you don't have to be a Texan to enjoy it.)

Until recently, cenizo was pretty much unknown among landscapers and nursery owners. Today, it's becoming fairly popular, primarily because it is attractive, evergreen, and, unlike many desert plants, not thorny.

Cenizo is native to the Chihuahuan desert, but it does well in other locales, as long as the conditions of full sun, well-drained soil, and mild winters (Zones 8–10) are present.

If you want to use cenizo in your landscape, remember that this is a desert plant. Give it plenty of sun and room. Mass it in a loose drift instead of lining it up in a tight row. Desert plants do not cram themselves together like those found in a Louisiana bottomland woods. They like plenty of light and air circulation. And please, do not overwater it.

Cenizo, when it is ill-used, is a truly pitiful sight. I've seen it growing scraggly and wispy under the shade of pecan trees, dead and drowned in heavy wet clays, lined up and overclipped under window sills until its twigs are almost bare of leaves.

I've also seen cenizo clipped into conventional-looking hedges. But I think it's prettier when you just give it a little pruning now and then and let it develop its own naturally soft, rounded shape. In this way, very old plants can reach ten feet in height and develop a twisting silvery trunk that is very lovely. Most cenizos sold at nurseries are compact selections that are unlikely to exceed four or five feet in height and can easily be maintained at two to three feet.

Use companion plants that are also drought-resistant; putting cenizo next to water-guzzlers like St. Augustine or Kentucky bluegrass is not a great idea. Asian jasmine, flowers that require weekly watering, and other plants that prefer more than thirty-five inches of rain a year do not belong near a cenizo either. Cenizo can thrive gloriously on twenty inches and sustain itself on a mere ten.

Take into consideration the aesthetics of leaf texture, foliage colors, and the shorter heights of plants associated with cenizo. Because cenizo has silvery leaves, use other plants that echo that color. Artemesia (there are various kinds), Arizona cypress, bursage (*Ambrosia* spp.), the silver-leaved form of agarito (*Mahonia trifoliolata*), and silver dalea (*Dalea bicolor* var. *argyraea*) are some good choices that are fairly easy to find.

For contrast, use plants with dark green foliage, such as evergreen sumac (*Rhus virens*), littleleaf sumac (*Rhus microphylla*), the large-leaved sumac called sugar bush (*Rhus ovata*), Texas mountain laurel (*Sophora secundiflora*), apache plume (*Fallugia paradoxa*), or creosote (*Larrea tridentata*). Mix in a few with yellow-green foliage like mesquite and goldenball lead tree (*Leucena retusa*) or those with lime-green trunks and branches such as paloverde and retama (*Parkinsonia* spp.).

At the base of your garden, use a mulch of local rocks; avoid lava rocks, dyed pebbles, or pea gravel. The idea is to look natural. And forget the black plastic underneath; you can plant a scattering of wildflowers or short tufts of native grass such as buffalograss, curly mesquite, or blue gramma among the rocks.

There are many flowers that look especially good with cenizo. Its own flowers are soft pink to lavender; one selection has white blooms. White-flowered perennials carry on the silvery color scheme, but my favorite combination includes orange, purple, red, and hot pink flowers for accents.

There are a variety of penstemons that bloom in early spring in reds and strong pinks. Later in the season, scarlet globemallow (*Sphaeralcea coccinea*) provides easy masses of bright orange-red satiny flowers that require only intermittent deep waterings to keep blooming all summer and fall.

You may be the first one on your block to plant cenizo, but, once your neighbors get a look at it, you won't be the last!

Grass Roots Support for Buffalograss

A while back, my husband and I were dining with friends, an unmarried couple I'll call John and Mary. They'd been dating for years with no hint of wedding bells—a situation that was clearly more vexing to Mary than to John. At one point in the evening's conversation, the topic of matrimony came up. I swear I didn't mention it; I'm not that crazy.

Well, one thing led to another, and soon John was feeling like a murdered heiress's sleazy-looking husband being grilled by Perry Mason. At one point, Mary just confronted him with the BIG question: "How come you're so afraid of commitment?" she asked.

John babbled on, offering one lame defense after another. Finally, he blurted out, "Okay, you want to know the real reason? It's my weekends! First, you get married. Then, you get a house. And that means a lawn! And that means mowing and watering and . . . and . . . that means my weekends will be ruined forever!"

I could have kept my mouth shut. But, no, I immediately and enthusiastically launched into a sales pitch for buffalograss, a turf grass that is becoming synonymous with low-maintenance. Buffalograss may not make lawnmowers obsolete, but they'll definitely be spending a lot more time in the tool shed. John's bachelor days were numbered!

Buffalograss (*Buchloe dactyloides*) was not named for the city in upstate New York. It was, instead, misnamed for those hairy mammals that once roamed our prairies (of course, we all know they're really bison). The confusion persists because no one can decide if it should be written as one word or two.

Buffalograss is native throughout the Great Plains, from Minnesota to Montana and south into Mexico—wherever conditions aren't too moist, too shady, or too sandy. Some of the newer varieties are being tested and used all over the country, from California to New Jersey. (A different type of buffalograss grows in Europe. My husband tells me that in his native Poland, there is a buffalograss vodka; a stalk of the grass is put into the bottle, giving the vodka a distinctive flavor and an amber hue. Some years back, the FDA outlawed the importation of this vodka because it feared that terrible little creatures would enter our country on the stalks. As if anything could live in that potent drink!)

In the right environment, maintaining a buffalograss lawn is a cinch. Make sure it gets a lot of sun, and give it just enough water in the summer to keep it green. You'll find that it needs less water than naturalized Bermuda and Kentucky bluegrass, and 50 to 80 percent less than is needed to keep St. Augustine alive and well. That's why water departments love buffalograss. It fits in perfectly with the new xeriscape concept.

Buffalograss is tough, and it can take a lot of foot traffic. At the same time, however, it's quite attractive, with a very pretty, fine, soft, even texture that invites bare feet. It covers quickly, needs less fertilizer, and outlives conventional turf grasses. It forms such a dense sod that weeds can't get a root in edgewise; pure stands in the wild are quite common. Furthermore, it stays out of your flowerbed; its roots are not at all invasive.

Buffalograss can be kept at a typical two-inch height, so as not to offend your neighbors, or it can be allowed to grow to its full eight to fifteen inches for use in a meadow. Or, for the more daring among you, as a beautifully undulating blue-green sea in front of your house. Most people let it grow to three or four inches and mow it just once or twice a year.

Come frost, or when the weather gets too dry, buffalograss will go dormant and turn a soft golden brown. The male flowers, a great part of its visual appeal, are visible even through the winter.

For years, the only buffalograss you could buy had been bred for pastures and had been selected for height, 'Texoka' and 'Sharp's Improved' being the best known. It's not that cattle don't like to stoop down; taller grass simply means more cow-chow per acre. These strains are excellent for use in meadows, but at one point water-conscious homeowners thought it would be a good idea to use them for lawns.

As sometimes happens when a good idea starts taking hold, the good idea gets even better. In the case of buffalograss, two new shorter varieties, 'Prairie' and '609,' are generating a great deal of interest in the turf community.

'Prairie' came on the market in July of 1990. Apple-green in the spring and summer and golden brown in the fall, it reaches a maximum height of four to six inches without supplemental watering. It was co-developed by Dr. M. C. Engelke, Associate Professor of Turf Grass Breeding and Management at the A&M Experiment Station in Dallas, and one of his students, Virginia Lehman. According to Dr. Engelke, 'Prairie,' a female strain, presents a more uniform, denser "lawn-like" appearance than the original varieties, because it eliminates the charming but less formal appearance of the male flowers waving above the turf. To keep it all female, this strain must be planted by sprigs, plugs, or sod, instead of seed.

'609' is Dr. Terry Riordan's baby. It was developed at the University of Nebraska and hit the market a few months after 'Prairie.' '609' is touted as having a somewhat darker, blue-green color and a denser mat.

Both grasses are extremely heat- and cold-resistant, drought-tolerant, and require minimal fertilization and pesticide control. Both spread rapidly and green earlier than St. Augustine and Bermuda. A bonus for hayfever sufferers: because both are female grasses, there's no pollen.

And, the development work goes on. A short-seeded variety, unnamed so far, is being developed by Dr. Riordan in Lincoln, Nebraska. Dr. Engelke has been testing it in Dallas since 1988, and he finds that it does well in our brand of summer heat.

Dr. David Huff, assistant professor of plant genetics at Rutgers University in New Jersey, tested many of these new varieties, and he found that they also do well in the wetter parts of the country. Huff is developing some unique strains:

a short-leaved buffalograss from Mexico—a diploid that should deliver greater density—and an all-male short turf variety that comes with different colored anthers; he already has red, white, and blue separated. Imagine *that* planted in front of the White House.

Admittedly, enthusiasm for buffalograss varies across the nation, from "the greatest thing since blue corn chips" here in the Southwest, to "promising, but the jury is still out" up north.

Connie and Glenn Suhren, in Garland, Texas, qualify as true believers. They broadcast 'Texoka' seed by hand in April of 1987, when their new house was surrounded by bare earth. Four months later, they had an attractive, verdant lawn. It probably would have spread more quickly in better soil, but the Suhrens had a lot of caliche in their yard.

To get it established, the Suhrens watered only twice a week (it was a particularly wet spring), and then cut back to just twice a month or whenever the soil felt dry. Normally, once established, buffalograss stays green on a couple of waterings a summer. Many of the Suhrens' neighbors, according to Connie, water their conventional lawns every other day.

Dr. David Northington, Director of the National Wildflower Research Center in Austin, Texas, has buffalograss around his home, too. He lives on a steep limestone slope where the soil is thin to nonexistent. He says he went on vacation one year and didn't water his lawn at all during July and August. When he got home, his lawn looked better than his neighbor's Bermuda, which had been watered twice a week. Imagine how much water this native buffalograss could save in states that suffer from water shortages.

In fact, the biggest problem buffalograss advocates face is convincing new users not to treat it in the same way as conventional turf grasses. They tend to overwater it, making it weedy. When they see that, they conclude that it isn't any good.

As for mowing (another big advantage for those of us who can easily think of several hundred other things we'd rather be doing), Glenn Suhrens cuts his lawn every three or four weeks, putting the mower on the highest setting. Connie claims the neighbors are out there every week cutting their Bermuda—sometimes more often.

Dr. Huff, at Rutgers, gives buffalograss a qualified thumbs up for the Northeast. He gives buffalograss high marks for toughness and low maintenance, particularly in compacted, heavy soils. He cites as an example an accidental plot that took hold on campus approximately ten years ago. It seems that another turf professor came to Rutgers from Oklahoma but decided not to pursue his buffalograss research in New Jersey, tossing his seeds into the nearest garbage dumpster. Well, not all of the seeds made it into the trash. Today, that plot of buffalograss is doing very well with no maintenance at all. According to Huff, the state of New Jersey is showing interest in using buffalograss along the Turnpike and the Garden State Parkway, on steep unmowable slopes.

Meanwhile, out west in Los Alamitos, California, Tom Buzbee with Kajima Engineering and Construction, Inc., is crediting 'Prairie' buffalograss with making his company's design for Cypress Golf Course possible.

The average golf course runs in the neighborhood of 160 acres, but Cypress had only 100 acres available. This required some fancy thinking layout-wise, fitting in all eighteen holes while keeping the golfers from killing each other with slices and hooks. The solution was a creative display of earth-moving and mound-building, effectively protecting each fairway from the others without having to resort to artificial screens and fences.

Buzbee reports that the precipitous slopes on the mounds make mowing difficult; they wanted to do it as seldom as possible, of course. Common Bermuda, the standard turf grass of America's courses, needs to be mowed once every five days; this buffalograss gets trimmed just once every five to six weeks!

Toss in the fact that California has been having more than its share of droughts of late, and you've got another reason why buffalograss was most welcome. The owners of the course are saving money on maintenance and water bills, and they're also setting a good ecological example for golf-course owners everywhere.

For many people around the country, especially those who live in the West and the Midwest, buffalograss will provide that low-maintenance lawn they've always wanted. But, is it the answer to every homeowner's dream? Obviously not. If your property is full of big shade trees, buffalograss won't make it; it needs lots of sun.

In the final analysis, the right lawn for you has to be determined by weighing all of the pros and cons of each turf grass in your region. When you select your turf grass, drought-tolerance and water needs should be considered, as well as cold-tolerance, soil types and conditions . . . and, of course, plain ol' visual appeal.

As for John and Mary . . . well, they eventually did get married. They bought a condo.

Mexican Hat:
A Black-thumb Perennial

You probably think that anyone who writes
a gardening book has to be a terrific gardener. I can't speak
for other authors, but I'm what is known as a black-thumb
gardener.

I definitely didn't get the right genes from my paternal
grandmother; now *she* was a gardener. She had the gift. The
touch. Granny would stick something into the ground, give it
a little water, and that was it. She never seemed to work very
hard at her gardening, yet year after year all kinds of flowers
and shrubs would flourish under her care. Even during
droughts. Nothing ever died by accident in Granny's garden.

My garden is quite different; death is not uncommon
here. The way I see it, if a plant can survive in spite of my
care, *anyone* can grow it successfully.

Mexican hat (*Ratibida columnaris*) is just such a plant.
It grows anywhere from Minnesota to, as you'd expect, Mexico. So right off you know it's tolerant of a wide range of
conditions. It starts blooming when it gets warm in the spring
and keeps on blooming until frost, and often blossoms even
after frost, until it gets knocked back by a hard freeze.

Mexican hat makes a good cut flower; it can last a week,
and the long slender stems make it easy to arrange. Each
flower is shaped like a sombrero, hence its name. The "brim"

has petals that are usually maroon around the base and yellow at the tips. Occasionally, the maroon part is orange or chocolate, and sometimes the petals are all yellow or all maroon. The tall, narrow cone, or "crown," of Mexican hat consists of the tiny yellow flowers that get fertilized to make seed. In the fall, the old cones that bloomed in late spring or early summer have turned gray, and you can easily crumble them to release dozens of ripe seeds.

These germinate easily, and one plant can provide enough to start a small meadow. To sow the seed: Scratch the soil lightly, scatter and cover them with soil to the thickness of the seed (about one millimeter), and then give the soil a gentle pat. If planted in the fall, the flowers will appear the first year.

The whole plant is normally vase-shaped, but this varies according to its environment. On rocky limestone slopes or in hot, unwatered sandy soils, it is about twelve to fourteen inches tall and well-shaped. It stays fresher and blooms longer if it is given afternoon shade but will probably not bloom in August and early September until the weather cools off or there is some rain.

In rich, irrigated garden soil, Mexican hat makes a luxuriant ferny mound two feet tall and two feet wide. In these conditions, it will bloom steadily throughout the hottest part of the summer. If it gets too much shade and moisture, it may develop mildew and become leggy. (Even easy plants have limits.) If the plant has endured drought, the top leaves will wither and new leaves will form at the base. This is how Mexican hat prefers to survive the winter.

However, without drought, the rich ferny mound is capable of staying green through a mild winter. If it dies in a harsh one, don't worry. Dozens of small plants should be on their way from seed that shattered in the fall on its own. If you are a basic pessimist, sow a little seed yourself each year after it has ripened.

If Mexican hat doesn't work for you—well, I understand they're doing wonderful things these days with plastic.

Putting Ferns in Their Proper Place

Think of ferns, and you probably think of indoor hanging baskets—restaurant decor or window dressing for your breakfast nook. Keep in mind that these ferns are imports from humid tropical climes. I've been in remarkably few restaurants or homes that qualify as suitable fern habitats. So, now you know why your ferns need a lot of tending and watering and spritzing—a degree of dedication I lack, which means my own ferns die at an alarming rate.

Besides, as one interior landscaper told me, "Mother Nature didn't make any indoor plants." And, that includes ferns. Ferns were meant to be outdoors, where they can provide marvelous accents and textures in your garden.

They can even serve as an attractive groundcover, if you live in a part of the country where they will receive ample moisture. Moisture is the key to success with ferns. In Canada—which is seldom confused with the tropics—you can find vast and lush fern carpets on the forest floors. What makes them lush is that they get plenty of moisture. And, because they're native to that area, they can handle the Canadian winters.

The ferns that will grow best for you are the ones that are native to your area—the very ones that are being ignored by the nursery trade and home gardeners alike.

You can find ferns growing naturally all over our country, in upland woods, in bogs, and alongside springs and waterways. The ones most usable for landscapes (those more than one foot tall) are native to areas that have an annual rainfall of more than thirty-five inches. Of course, you'll find equally large ferns in areas with less rainfall, but in those cases the temperatures tend to be lower to compensate.

Believe it or not, you can find ferns in the desert, too, although they aren't really growing in the desert habitat itself; they are clinging to canyon walls where they find dependable seeps, shaded by cliffs or woodland. Those ferns that grow where the seeps are shallow and dependent on rainfall grow small, about the size of your hand. And, even though these ferns are a delight to discover on a nature hike, they aren't really suitable for most gardens.

Some ferns are more drought-tolerant than others, but they are all vulnerable to drought to some degree, and that's because they're so shallow-rooted. When a drought occurs and ferns get too dry, they are programmed to go dormant and wait for better and wetter days. If dry conditions persist, a few ferns in the colony will actually die; the whole colony can die if the drought goes on all summer.

Most ferns grow in colonies because they reproduce easily by the roots. They can even be somewhat aggressive when conditions are properly moist and cool. A healthy colony of ferns can advance approximately one foot each year—this is important to know when you are buying only a few ferns and you want them to fill a larger space.

Ferns are notoriously hard to transplant, but talented gardeners can get them started in the greenhouse from root cuttings. When ferns are grown from spores, the process is much slower. Each fern releases millions of microscopic spores each year in late summer. On a dry, breezy day, the spores float out into the world, hoping to find a moist shady spot.

The tiny fraction that are successful are still a long way from becoming ferns. First, they have to grow gametophytes, quarter-inch heart-shaped plants that also have to grow, producing a fertile egg. Only a few of these eggs live long enough to develop successfully into adults. How's that for a precarious and convoluted method of reproduction!

Nurseries that stock outdoor ferns usually have a pretty dismal selection—one or two kinds—and, all too often, one of those choices is probably from Japan. That's a shame. We have so many lovely native ferns, with a wide range of heights, textures, and habits. Some are very polite; others will seize an acre and make it their own.

In order to describe some of the most hardy and wide-spread of these ferns to you, I will divide them into two groups: those that can grow in shallow water and tight clay soils and can tolerate poor drainage, and those that require plenty of moisture but good drainage and lots of oxygen at the same time, growing only in sandy loam or on rocky slopes.

Poor drainage ferns are the easiest to grow. You need only worry about whether or not they are getting enough wa-ter, *not* that they are receiving too much. These ferns may be planted around the edge of a pond, under a bird bath, and in those areas around the foundation of your house where moss appears on its own. In a typically level garden, you can dig out a shallow hollow to plant them in. Then, watering is a snap; just let the hose run until the hollow is filled. Repeat only when the soil becomes almost dry. A top dressing of com-posted manure is a good idea; it feeds the roots and helps hold in moisture.

The two Osmunda ferns are the largest and most distinc-tive. Cinnamon fern, *Osmunda cinnamomea,* is two to five feet tall and will grow as wide. It is native from Newfound-land to New Mexico. The roots gradually make huge mounds of osmunda fiber that stick up out of the bog. These ferns can grow to be very old. In fact, one source I read implied that they might be "immortal." The leaves are twice cut, which means the overall effect is fine textured. The fertile fronds are cinnamon in color.

Royal fern, *Osmunda regalis* var. *spectabilis,* gets three to six feet tall. It is native from Canada to South America. It is most often found just out of the bog, on the squishy banks above the cinnamon ferns. It grows very well in a garden setting and, because of its height, it makes a dramatic back-drop for smaller ferns. Place one or more together to form a clump in a corner where you need more height. The leaves are of a coarser texture, only once divided, and the fertile fronds are gold.

Lady fern, *Athyrium filix-femina* grows two to six feet high. It can be fairly aggressive and makes a good groundcover. Its height makes it useful around a deck, or as a prominent mass at the end of the garden. The leaves are finely divided to give the fronds a lacy appearance. It has varieties native to both western and eastern North America.

Chain fern, *Woodwardia areolata* (still called *Lorinseria areolata* by some botanists), is one of my favorites. It's usually only about a foot tall, although it can reach two and one-half feet in very rich soil. It has a very simple leaf and makes a soothing groundcover, perfect for setting off the taller, more richly textured ferns. I often see this fern growing on the soggy slopes around the royal fern. It is native to all of eastern North America.

These ferns, each with its own height and texture, are especially pretty when combined with one another.

Good drainage ferns do best in rocky or sandy soils, in raised beds, or on slopes, as they cannot tolerate standing water or soggy soils. If they grow in water, that water must be constantly moving and freshly laden with air. These ferns are considerably more drought-tolerant than the bog ferns, but that's a relative statement; they can never be allowed to dry out completely without the risk of loss. Don't plan to use these as a groundcover in unwatered situations, unless you live in the mountains or so far north that summer temperatures rarely get over 90°F.

Sensitive fern, *Onoclea sensibilis,* is often called sympathy fern, a name that acknowledges its tendency to curl its fronds when touched. It's also called bead fern, the "beads" referring to spikes laden with beadlike spore sacs that remain after the leaves have frozen to the ground in winter. Sensitive fern prefers loose, sandy soils and is always seen on the sloping sides of wet places. It is one foot tall in regular garden soil and might reach three feet in heavily composted beds. It has a very coarse texture, so it is usually best used farther from the house. It can be fairly aggressive, which means it makes an easy groundcover for large spaces. It is native from eastern Canada west to Saskatchewan and south to the Gulf of Mexico.

There are two predominant maidenhair ferns in the United States. Both are native from coast to coast. *Adiantum capillus-veneris* is the southern one, native from Virginia to California. *Adiantum pedatum* is northern. Both have wiry black stems and small, distinctive fan-shaped leaflets. The big visual difference is the stem: the northern one forms a gentle swirl. In the Southwest, maidenhair fern is seen only on lime-stone ledges or cave walls that have a continuous flow of water. It seeds out (or spores out) beautifully down moist limestone retaining walls and loves the humidity created by a waterfall. I've seen both grown successfully in moist, raised beds where they can form very luxuriant colonies.

Polystichums are mostly evergreen ferns. Christmas fern, *Polystichum acrostichoides,* is native from Nova Scotia to Wisconsin to Mexico. Its fronds are a darker green and a sim-pler design than most ferns. They bunch together to make dense clumps one to two feet tall and just as broad. Consistent moisture and super drainage are musts, but if you need an evergreen fern of short stature for around the house, then it's worth a little extra trouble.

In the Pacific Northwest, there are eight species of *Polystichum.* The most common and easy to grow is sword fern (*P. munitum*), which makes magnificent three- to five-foot-tall clumps in lowland conifer forests. Not only is it larger and lusher than Christmas fern, its leaflets are so densely ar-ranged that it has a fringed look. A popular and more compact version is called the sun fern.

Bracken, *Pteridium aquilinum* var. *pseudocaudatum,* is the oddball of the fern family. One species populates most of the world. Unlike the other ferns, its roots grow deep. It is most often found in poor soils and in hotter, drier conditions than other ferns can tolerate. It prefers well-drained, poor, sandy, acidic soils, although it can grow in a wide range of conditions, giving itself the reputation as the "weedy" fern. It is commonly two to three feet tall and forms large, coarse colonies. Because it is not as delicate and well-behaved as the other ferns I've described, most gardeners would not think of using it. Yet, if you're in the Deep South, and you need masses of fern deep in an unwatered wood, this is the only one likely to work for you.

The best known fern in the South, and the only one easily bought at many nurseries, is the wood fern (*Thelypteris kun-thii*). This is one of our most drought-tolerant ferns; it can thrive with only one watering a week, given sufficient shade and temperatures below 100°F. It can grow in any soil, acid or limey. However, wood fern is also one of the least winter-hardy ferns. It definitely suffers in areas where temperatures fall below 0°F.

I'm not advocating tossing all your fern baskets away. If you've got the dedication and desire to keep them alive, more power to you. But, if you live in a fern-friendly environment and you'd like to add an exotic touch to your garden, give your native ferns a try. I haven't met anyone yet who's been sorry they did.

Sumacs for Red Fall Color

You yankees have so much glorious fall color up there (as my Yankee husband keeps reminding me), you probably don't give your sumacs their full due. But, down here in the South, where it doesn't always get cold enough to produce such startling foliage, we appreciate them like crazy.

That's not to say our native trees don't give us some really lovely autumn displays; they deliver a lot of golds, reds, and yellows. The trouble is the color is rationed out in small doses over a two-month period instead of being squeezed into one or two breathtaking weeks. The satisfaction quotient just isn't the same.

So, for a guaranteed bit of autumn glory, we plant sumacs. They are the South's most brilliant and dependable red fall color. Here are descriptions of a small tree, a thicket, and a shrub you ought to know about:

Prairie flameleaf sumac (*Rhus lanceolata*) is a lovely small (ten to twenty feet) tree native to Texas and New Mexico. Its slender pale gray trunk is smooth and covered with white dots. This tree flowers in late summer, displaying creamy white pyramids of blooms that are usually covered with butterflies. The fruits are clusters of tiny hard red berries that have a lemony flavor and are eaten by a number of birds.

When you plant it, remember that it needs full sun. It isn't terribly picky about soil; it can prosper in sand, loam, caliche, clay, or limestone—as long as it is well-drained. Suggestion: plant it in front of a yellow-leafed soapberry, another native tree. The color combination is lovely when they turn together, which is likely.

The prairie flameleaf is often considered just a variety of the flameleaf sumac (*Rhus copallina*), which is similar in every way, except that it is more tolerant of shade and damper soils. It is native from New England to Illinois south to the Gulf of Mexico.

The smooth sumac (*Rhus glabra*) is a thicket, and it grows from three to ten feet tall. Now, I'll admit that it can be a pest if you don't put it in the right place; it *always* suckers. I had one travel twenty feet under a deck and then come up in a flower garden, where it was most unwelcome. It's native throughout the United States, except in the deserts.

Its natural habitat is the sunny edge of a woods. As the woods grow out and the shade extends, it travels as a thicket to maintain its position in the sun. Smooth sumac is ideal for holding an eroding slope or for creating a bird habitat in the corner of a large back yard. It grows very quickly. I've known it to start suckering only one month after being planted.

The leaves of the two flameleaf sumacs (trees) and the smooth sumac (a shrub) are very similar. And, since you'd be buying them when both are small (in one- to five-gallon containers), you'll want to know which is which. Look carefully at the leaves. The tree leaf consists of a stem with numerous pairs of leaflets. You'll also see a row of tiny (one-eighth to one-fourth inch) leafy material running along both sides of the stem. The smooth sumac doesn't have these leafy margins on the stem. That's not why it's called smooth sumac, by the way; the name comes from its smooth, shiny leaves.

Our shortest sumac is the shrubby aromatic sumac (*Rhus trilobata* with its varieties, including *Rhus aromatica*, also called *Rhus trilobata* var. *aromatica*). The group, as a whole, is native from the Atlantic to the Pacific and from Canada to Mexico. It doesn't look like the others at all because its leaflets are arranged in threes, and the whole leaf is usually only two or three inches broad. It normally forms a well-rounded shrub about three feet tall, although I've seen old ones reach eight feet, and twelve feet has been recorded. You can use it as a single plant, but I think it's most effective

Prairie Flameleaf Sumac
Rhus lanceolata

when clustered to give a thicket effect. The beauty of it is that it makes a controllable thicket because it doesn't sucker.

This sumac will tolerate the most shade of all those described here. In full sun, it becomes a brilliant red. In six hours or less, it will turn yellow and orange with touches of red. Sometimes the leaves are glossy, but usually they are fuzzy, as are the fruits.

Aromatic sumac blossoms quite early in the spring with little yellow flowers; the berries ripen red in early summer and are prime bird food. Its name comes from the rather spicy fragrance you get from crushing the leaves.

If you can't find a sumac to buy at a nursery and you plan to dig one from the wild, don't even touch it until you are sure you have identified the sumac correctly. I don't mean to sound overly dramatic, but aromatic sumac has a leaf composed of three leaflets very similar to poison ivy and poison oak. The difference is that the lobes found on the aromatic sumac are only at the ends of the leaflets. The smooth sumac's leaf is similar to that of poison sumac. Poison sumac has fewer leaflets, but when you are looking at eleven to thirteen leaflets, it may be either one. If you see the leafy stem of the flameleaf sumacs, you are quite safe. None of the sumacs I have recommended here will give you any kind of rash.

Our Unsung Horticultural Heroes

❧

True or false: It's a lot easier these days to find native plants in nurseries.

The answer is true. Before the mid-eighties, your average nursery carried only a few native shade trees; that was about all. Today, many of these same nurseries will have at least a small sampling of native perennials, shrubs, ornamental trees, and even groundcovers. There is a growing list of specialty nurseries in most states that devote at least half of their stock to a wide selection of native plants.

This expansion is happening because public demand is increasing. But, it's also occurring because now there are a large number of commercial wholesale growers willing to take on the challenges and problems inherent in entering this new industry on the ground floor.

That anyone gets into this business in the first place is remarkable. There may be tougher ways to make a living, but I'd be hard pressed to list many. The successful grower must have, in equal measure, the green thumb of Luther Burbank, the financial acumen of J. P. Morgan, and the mind-reading skills of The Amazing Kreskin.

At this time, most of our non-native nursery stock is grown in California, Louisiana, and Tennessee. The grower purchases seed and cuttings that have gone through an extensive selection process; sometimes this involves hand-pollinated breeding or hybridization. And, the main thing we must understand is that, almost always, these selections have taken place in Japanese or European test fields, where the climate and soil differ greatly from most parts of our country. This is why nurseries do such a good business replacing plants that die in our late freezes and summer dry spells.

It makes sense for us not only to start using more natives, but also to start growing our own well-adapted natives to supply an ever-increasing demand.

Easier said than done. Starting a new industry is never a piece of cake, but try it in today's financial climate— companies, large and small, are going belly up faster than bougainvillea in a blue norther!

We must develop test plots for our native plants. The only one we currently have in Texas (and one of the very few in the entire country) is at the Texas A&M facility in North Dallas. Research scientist Benny J. Simpson is working with native trees and shrubs and has developed and released several selections: 'White Storm,' a pure white desert willow and 'Dark Storm,' a two-tone burgundy and rose one, 'Mount Emory,' a mountain sage (*Salvia regla*), and five cenizos (the Cloud series).

These, and his many other selections, are based on almost twenty years of hard work. Simpson makes several trips a year, combing the state for attractive plants. He marks desirable plants when they are in bloom, fall color, or fruit. Then, he often has to make a return trip to gather seed or to take cuttings at the optimum time of year. He then must figure out how to get the seeds to germinate. After he has seedlings, he plants them in test rows and watches them. It takes years of observation to winnow out those that have the most drought-resistance, cold-hardiness, and beauty.

Once a particular plant is selected and named, it becomes available to growers. Nursery owners can purchase cuttings from these selections for a nominal price and save themselves a lot of hassle.

Most states don't have this advantage. In Phoenix, Arizona, Ron Gass, a wholesale nurseryman and owner of Mountain States Nursery, uses as many of Simpson's selections from the Chihuahuan Desert as are applicable for the Sonoran and Mojave deserts where he makes most of his sales. But, to offer a wide range of desert plants, Gass must scout and select and test just like Simpson does, but at his own expense.

The time alone involved in a process like this is staggering. Suppose you've decided to grow Eve's necklace (*Sophora affinis*). You have to schedule a trip in the spring to find a community of trees where the color is a rich, pretty pink, and locate the clusters that are exceptionally large and luscious, making six- to nine-inch-long necklaces of black-beaded seeds. Eve's necklace with short, dirty-white clusters and short necklaces are not going to capture the hearts of the buying public.

Then, if you want to sell to nurseries far from home—even in other states—you must make sure that the stock you've selected is adaptable to that large market. Or, you need to gather from more than one source.

For example, let's suppose you're a grower in Tennessee with a good sense of ethics and you have orders from all over the United States for chinquapin oak (*Quercus muhlenbergii*), a lovely oak with long scalloped leaves with a preference for limestone soils. Oaks can be grown only from seed and this seed must be fresh off the tree and perfectly ripe; timing for harvesting, therefore, is crucial. If you gather all of your acorns in and around Tennessee, the plants won't be winter-hardy in Wisconsin, or drought-tolerant in Texas. To sell widely with a clear conscience, you need to gather seed in those states as well, and keep the seed separate and the trees labeled according to provenance.

That's just the beginning of your problems. How are you going to know when the acorns are ripe in Wisconsin and Texas? And, how will you be able to afford that kind of travel expense? Here in Texas, it's possible for a grower to take off the exact same weekend he did the year before and drive hundreds of miles for ripe seed—only to discover he's arrived two weeks late or one week early. Weather varies each year, and so does the exact date of ripening.

Even when you have the seed, things don't always go well. One year, Mary Buchanan of Texas Star Gardens in Abilene planted hundreds of chinquapin oaks for the Texas market. Each morning, when she visited her greenhouse, there were fewer acorns. Were they rotting without a trace? No, squirrels had chewed a tiny hole in a corner of the greenhouse and were coming for a midnight raid. Mary discovered the hole, closed it up, gathered more acorns, and tried again.

Then, she discovered that she had a double crop. Chinquapin acorns were sprouting everywhere; the squirrels had planted them in the dirt floor, in pots of perennials, in pipes, even in an old shoe.

But, squirrels are the least of your problems. Seed almost always has to be fumigated; even as you gather it, you are gathering countless insects that feast on those seeds and will continue to chomp away until you get rid of them.

Many seeds are not easy to germinate. They require cold, light, darkness, acid baths, or combinations of these treatments, and timing is important. Creosote (*Larrea tridentata*), the most important evergreen shrub of the southwestern deserts, was not used in cultivated landscapes until very recently because no one could figure out how to propagate it. Dr. Jimmy Tipton finally discovered the secret when he was at the Texas Agricultural Experiment Station in El Paso. In 1990, Ron Gass finally figured out how to germinate the seed in a way that made it possible for creosote to be grown in mass for the nursery trade. Coldenia (*Tiquilia greggii*) is a delightful silver and purple shrub-flower of the deserts that is still unavailable because no one has been able to crack its germination code, as of this writing.

The other major way to grow plants is from cuttings, and that, of course, is another can of worms. For the highest rate of success, you'll need a mist bench; a sophisticated system that recreates a humid, rain-forest-like environment for the cuttings.

This can be an expensive investment for a grower just starting out. Some flowers, like that charming bedding plant known as blackfoot daisy (*Melampodium leucanthum*), can't be grown commercially without a mist bench.

To be successful with cuttings, you also have to know whether green soft shoots or hard woody ones root best for each specific plant. If it's hardwood cuttings, do they respond more readily if taken in the summer? The fall? When the plant is dormant? Hormones can greatly affect rate of growth—but which ones, and how much? The variables seem endless.

Now, let's imagine that you've mastered all of these obstacles. Finally, your seed is sown in flats and is coming up, the cuttings are leafed out and putting on new growth and you're home free. You wish!

Now you have to figure out what kind of soil mix to use. Most growers have sprinkler systems that water several times a day—far too much for a drought-tolerant plant. So, you pot the plant in a light, fast-draining soil mix. This is fine until you ship it to your customer, a retail nursery that can't water as much as you do. So your soil mix will dry out, and the drought-tolerant plant will turn brown and crispy. Your phone starts ringing.

Solutions are, of course, being found by dedicated growers willing to search for them. Heidi Sheesley of Tree Search Farms in Houston uses a standard soil mix, but then she puts each kind of native tree on its own drip line, giving it just the amount of water it needs.

Dorothy Mattiza of Gunsight Mountain Ranch and Nursery in Tarpley, Texas, has been mixing real soil in her pots, so that her plants transplant especially well into heavy clay or rocky soils. This is not, however, an ideal solution; the soil makes the pots too heavy for easy handling and shipping. She also feels as if she were selling off her ranch one potful at a time.

Correct fertilization is another gray area for native plants. For the most part, they prefer less fertilizer than conventional plants, but each grower must discover for himself how much or how little to use to get maximum growth for the least cost.

After all of this, you still face the problem of educating the nurseries you want to sell to, most of whom have never heard of you or your natives. Their salespeople need to know what native plants they'll be selling, how to display them properly, and how to care for them. They also need to know precisely which natives are best for their area and how to intelligently answer questions from the buying public.

Ah, yes, there's the public. This part of the business will really test your mettle, as you try to anticipate what they will want next year. If you have a demand for Turk's cap (*Malvaviscus arboreus* var. *drummondii*) this year and sell all that you can grow, you may not be able to give it away next year.

Even though these specific examples are from nurseries I am personally acquainted with here in Texas, rest assured that the difficulties are universal; they affect native plant growers all over the country. But then, nobody said it was easy being a pioneer.

The next time you go to buy a native plant, you'll have a better chance of finding what you want than you would have had a few years ago, thanks to the perseverance and dedication of those noble, unsung botanical heroes and heroines, the commercial native-plant growers.

Observations

I went to the woods because I wished to live deliberately, to front only the essential facts of life, and see if I could not learn what it had to teach, and not, when I came to die, discover that I had not lived.

HENRY THOREAU
Walden

Chili Piquin
Capsicum frutescens

Rediscovering Our Lost Native Herbs

How many native American herbs can you name? If you know more than two, congratulations; even expert herbalists have trouble in this area. We simply have no idea how many culinary and medicinal herbs we have. Much of this knowledge—the culmination of millenia of exploration and experimentation—has been lost along with our Native American cultures. Today, there are still a few medicine men and women who can relate herbal lore that was orally handed down to them, but even that is scattered and fragmented. How different it was in other parts of the world.

Herbs have been an integral part of humanity since prehistoric times. Oregano was discovered by anthropologists in European interglacial human deposits that were 160,000 years old. Ancient Greeks, Romans, and Egyptians used herbs extensively, such as parsley, rosemary, thyme, sage, marjoram, coriander (cilantro), dill, and garlic. And, cumin is mentioned in the Bible.

The ancient Mediterraneans defined "herb" more loosely than we do today. Along with perennials, they considered trees and grasses to be herbs, as long as the bark, leaves, flowers, roots, or fruits could be used for medicines, flavorings, teas, or fragrances. For example, they considered roses to be important herbs and used them as salve, perfume, flavoring in puddings—and as a cure for hangovers. Their traditions are still our traditions. Today, we use rose water for flavoring foods, attar of roses for perfumes, and rose hips for teas. In fact, modern medicine employs rose hips in many of our prescription drugs.

Because much of our culture is derived from that of Europe, it's only natural that these European herbs are the ones we're most familiar with; our spice racks and grocery shelves, not surprisingly, reflect the predominance of Mediterranean herbs. The same is true of our typical herb garden.

If you'd like your herb garden and your spice rack to go beyond the typical, then I suggest you take a look at some of our own native—and underutilized—herbs.

The current trend in herb gardening is the emphasis on the culinary, rather than the medicinal, properties of herbs. The aesthetic appeal of the herb garden is also becoming more important. It not only has to be useful and emit the spicy scent of aromatic leaves, today's herb garden must also have eye appeal.

The native herbs I will describe for you here meet all of the above requirements. Like Mediterranean herbs, they require good drainage, so plant them in a sloping bed, or in a well-prepared, raised bed. Most herbs prefer alkaline soil, so if you have very acidic soil, add lime. Bonemeal is a good fertilizer.

Water sparingly for a more pungent flavor; a dryish soil causes the leaves to possess a higher proportion of aromatic oil. Herb leaves contain oil, as well as water, as a defense against drought; oil will not evaporate out of the leaf in the same way water will.

You may find that some of our herbs are more drought-tolerant than Mediterranean herbs. Most of the United States has higher temperatures and longer periods of high evaporation. If you have been consistently losing a traditional herb in a particularly hot, sunny spot, try a native American herb. Here are a few I like:

Salvia. Use the leaves in stuffings, salad oils, soups, cheeses, or in potpourris. Flowers are good in salads or for garnish.
    Salvia is the official botanical name for sage. The one you're probably familiar with is *Salvia officinalis,* the Mediterranean purple-flowered sage that has been used in

Western medicine and cooking for thousands of years. Our native salvias have a similar flavor.

The natives show quite a variety of growth habits. Some are shrubby, and they grow only about a foot tall. Mejorana de Pais (*Salvia ballotaeflora*), a blue salvia from Mexico that slips over the border into Texas and New Mexico, and is surprisingly winter-hardy down to −5°F., can grow as high as six feet. Others are perennials, ranging from eighteen inches to five feet tall. Cedar sage (*Salvia roemeriana*) can make a mat of evergreen foliage less than six inches tall. Salvias are mostly red to hot pink, although blue, purple, pale pink, and white are not uncommon. Most tend to bloom during the entire warm season, but peak bloom time for many is in late summer and early fall, when hummingbirds migrate.

I find that the palatability of the leaves varies considerably during the summer, so always taste-test before you use salvia—especially if the boss is coming home for dinner. From my own personal leaf-tasting sessions, I find that the red-flowered salvias are usually very nicely flavored, while the blue ones, although pleasantly aromatic, tend to be bitter.

My favorite red salvias for culinary purposes are autumn sage, mountain sage, scarlet sage, and cedar sage.

Autumn sage (*Salvia greggii*) is the easiest to find and buy. It likes very good drainage, even moisture, and full sun, although it will tolerate a half day of sunshine. In a heavy clay soil, it is easier to grow on a slope or in a big clay pot. It comes in red, purple, coral, white, and hot pink. "Autumn sage" is something of a misnomer. It blooms big in the fall but also puts on a stupendous show in April, and it gives fairly steady color throughout the summer. When blooms slack off, snip off the old bloom stalks so it will start blooming again. It freezes around 0°F.

Mountain sage (*Salvia regla*) is similar in size and habits to the autumn sage, but it really does bloom just in the autumn. It has rounded crinkly leaves with scalloped edges, and the flowers are a beautiful cherry red.

Scarlet sage (*Salvia coccinea*) is best treated as an annual in Zone 8 and further north. It thinks any old soil is great, and it loves extra moisture but is tolerant of severe drought. It starts blooming in the spring, gradually gathering speed all summer, and really is gorgeous in the fall, often even after Christmas.

This sage can get tall and lanky in the shade but responds well to being mowed or frequently snipped. In the sun, it is naturally thick and bushy, growing to about thirty inches tall by the first freeze. It also comes in a lovely shade of pure pink; I've even seen a white one, but that color is rare. When it gets frozen to the ground, cut off the brown stalk and shake the seed out on the ground. The old plant might not return in the spring. A winter mulch of leaves is helpful to protect the roots.

Cedar sage (*Salvia roemeriana*) is my favorite. It is less than a foot tall, takes full sun or heavy dappled shade, such as under a cedar tree, and is evergreen. Let it reseed freely, as it is a fairly short-lived perennial. The flowers are a deep clear red and usually bloom once in the spring, once in the summer, and once in the fall. It thrives in a variety of soils, mingles beautifully with rocks, and makes a luxuriant low-growing pot plant. All it requires is good drainage and a winter above 0°F.

Don't get these sages mixed up with the silver-leafed desert sages; sand sage, wormwood, and sagebrush are all artemisias. They have a wonderful aromatic smell but taste very strong and bitter, and more than one leaf can overpower and ruin any culinary effort. "Texas sage" usually refers to cenizo, a *Leucophyllum,* still another silver-leafed "sage," which seems to have some medicinal properties but is *not* recommended for cooking.

Monarda. Use leaves as seasoning, in teas, or for garnish. Use flowers in sauces or for garnish.

Bergamot (*Monarda fistulosa*) is a perennial that spreads by the roots. In winter, it is a four-inch high mat of mint-fragrant leaves. By late spring, when it starts blooming, it is one and one-half to four feet tall, depending on how rich and deep your soil is and how much moisture it gets. Because it loses its root-shading rosette leaves, it needs a good mulch in the summer to keep it from going dormant. With afternoon shade and watering, it might bloom all summer. The flowers are pale pink to pale lavender and smell as minty as the leaves.

The Rocky Mountain version of this mint (*M. fistulosa* var. *menthaefolia*) has a different flavor and is often called wild oregano. It can be used instead of grocery store (Greek) oregano. Michael Moore, in his excellent book, *Medicinal Plants of the Mountain West,* says that the spicy flowers are nice in chili dishes.

The similar-looking red bergamot, *Monarda didyma,* is used to flavor Earl Grey tea. This lovely mint, also called beebalm or Oswego tea, is native to the Appalachian mountains and is used widely in gardens where the summers are not too hot and dry.

Limoncillo. Use in teas (good for colds), as a seasoning, or as a garnish.

Limoncillo (*Pectis angustifolia*) is a charming, low-growing Western annual, native from Nebraska west to the eastern side of the Rockies, up to about 10,000 feet in Colorado, and south to Texas and Mexico.

It prefers sandy or rocky soils. Plant the seed in fall or in spring, after the danger of frost has passed. Starting in summer, the lemon-scented leaves will be covered with tiny golden-yellow daisies. Limoncillo is visually used to its best effect if allowed to drape itself over a wall, over the edge of a patio pot, or between stepping stones.

Chili piquin. Use as you would jalapeños.

Chili piquin (*Capsicum frutescens*) is also called bird pepper because the tiny ripe red peppers are very popular with birds. This is the original chili pepper, native from Arizona to southern Florida and throughout tropical America. Where temperatures rarely dip below freezing, chili piquin is an evergreen shrub that bears flowers and chilis most of the year. Further north, it might freeze back to the roots or reseed as an annual. It thrives in dappled shade.

Licorice. Chew on naturally sweet roots, raw or dried. Can also be used as a tea.

Licorice (*Glycyrrhiza lepidota*) is close kin to *Glycyrrhiza glabra,* the Zone 9 Mediterranean herb used to flavor licorice candy and cough syrups. Ours is far more cold-tolerant, native all over the American West from British Columbia to Mexico. It is found mostly in sandy arroyos and roadside ditches. The plant is rather pretty, usually about two feet tall, with spikes of creamy blossoms followed by velcro-textured pea pods. The leaves are light green and compound, a characteristic typical of the pea family.

This perennial goes dormant at frost, the best time to dig the roots. Don't worry about digging up your whole plant; it suckers like mad. Harvesting copious amounts of the roots each year is the only way to control it in the garden. Dig down at least eighteen inches to get to the best roots. Be sure to plant it in the sand it likes, then digging it each fall will not become a formidable job.

There are dozens of other herbs the Native Americans used; you can learn about them in any number of good books about medicinal uses. I have been extremely conservative on this list for culinary use, as Native American dishes may taste rather strange to modern palates. Everything here, however, I have tasted myself, with the exception of the licorice, which I abhor!

Watch the Birdies
Instead of the Soaps

Not too long ago, my husband and I were researching retirement homes for his mom. At each one, a sales representative proudly showed us the accommodations, the dining room, and all of the recreational facilities, from libraries to television rooms to arts-and-crafts areas.

It was all new to me; my grandmother had lived to a ripe old age in her own home, tending her garden almost until the end. One of her greatest joys was to watch the birds that were attracted to the garden.

It occurred to me that many of the residents in these retirement and nursing homes might also be avid bird-watchers, and that for a number of them who were confined to their beds, bird-watching at their windows might offer an exciting and refreshing change of pace from the intellectual stimuli of "Jeopardy" and "The Days of Our Lives."

At this point I should mention, for the benefit of sympathetic but cost-conscious administrators, attracting birds is relatively simple and inexpensive. A bird bath and a squirrel-proof sunflower seed dispenser are very effective for bringing in sparrows and starlings and won't hurt a budget already straining from too many needs and too few dollars.

If you want to get a bit more sophisticated and attract nesting mockingbirds, cardinals, and bluejays, you're going to have to put in a few carefully chosen plants. Different parts of the country will, of course, have various options. The ones I mention below are excellent choices for most of the Southeast, and as far west as Texas.

A Bird Garden:

- Select a spot fairly close to and easily visible from a main sitting area, such as a communal sitting porch, or outside the picture window of a dining or community room. A courtyard surrounded by many bedrooms with big windows is also effective.
- Mark off an "island" of at least thirty feet by fifteen feet. This will be the bird garden.
- Clear the island of lawn grasses.
- Surround its edges with a simple, unmortared stone wall, two stones high *or* with neatly cut sticks and branches left over from pruning. Either setting provides an environment for little insects and lizards, as well as other small creatures. These are summer snacks for the birds and, without them, the birds will be less likely to appear or stay around.
- This point is very important: Do not—I repeat, do not—use any poisons in this garden; you'll end up poisoning the birds that you are trying to feed.
- If your island is in full sun, plant either a female yaupon holly, female possumhaw, or female wax myrtle for winter fruit as well as a sumac, female persimmon, or fruit tree for fall fruit on the south or west end of the island. On the north or east end, plant a tiny meadow using sideoats grama and a regional wildflower mix or plant a perennial garden of native flowers that you can purchase as plants from the nursery. Use lots of salvias and daisies.
- If your island is fairly shady, choose an evergreen such as cherry laurel, a female yaupon, a female cedar, or, if you live in Zones 9 or 10, an anacua. Then, add a bird-fruit tree such as Carolina buckthorn or viburnum. Use Turk's cap, pigeon berry, or inland seaoats as a groundcover.
- Out in the open, away from the island and any trees but in easy view, place a bird bath. It is important for the bird bath to be in an open space so cats and other predators can't hide within pouncing range.

Maintenance is easy; some of the more sprightly senior citizens should be able to do it themselves. In fact, I wouldn't be surprised if being on the bird-garden crew doesn't become a mark of distinction, sort of like being the blackboard monitor back in grade school.

The duties involved are simple and require very little effort: Fill the bird bath every day and make sure it's clean. Pull out ugly weeds and grasses that could overtake the pretty flowers and selected grasses. And, again, keep the hired maintenance crews from using any poisons on the plants in the island. If a maintenance person is spotted approaching with a spray bottle of toxic weed killer or insecticide, I'm told a cane waving in the air can be a marvelous deterrent.

Things That Go Bump in the Spring

ᳵ

Every spring, we hear a familiar and very unpleasant sound around our house: a loud thump against a window pane. We cringe, knowing what that sound means, and we rush outside. There, sprawled beneath the window lies a cedar waxwing, a bird easily identified by its soft pale yellow belly, black mask, crest, and distinctive yellow band on the end of the tail. There's also a small red waxy tip on each wing, which accounts for its name.

The bird is not dead, it's merely knocked senseless after flying full-tilt into the window. Usually, the bird needs only a few minutes to pull itself together, and we give it that chance, rounding up all of our cats and putting them in the house. Our daughter, Melissa, stands guard over the dazed bird until it can fly off again.

We used to speculate on why this happens so often and so predictably. Did these waxwings flunk navigation in flight school? Are they simply mentally deficient? Do they have poor eyesight? The answer is . . . they're pickled! Looped! Soused!

Twice each year these waxwings fly through our part of Texas. In the fall, they escape the coming cold and travel to their winter vacation spots down south. Heading south, they are a sober lot. But in the spring, on their way back north to their nesting sites, they turn into rambunctious party animals.

One last fling before beginning the serious business of raising families, I guess.

And, where does the party begin? At the nearest possumhaw—the fruits have fermented nicely over the winter, and the waxwings know it.

The possumhaw (*Ilex decidua*) is a fifteen- or twenty-foot multitrunked holly tree that looks very much like the yaupon holly in the summer. However, in the winter it sheds its leaves, leaving the female loaded with colorful red to yellow fruit. The lack of leaves makes it much showier than the closely related female yaupon.

The fruits ripen just as winter migration begins, but only a few get eaten at this time. One theory suggests that birds rank fresh possumhaw berries fairly low on their list of favorite nibbles; they'll dine on them only when tastier treats are unavailable.

Personally, I favor another theory: these waxwings are no dummies. They know that possumhaw berries, unlike other fruits that drop off before spring, will last through the winter. So, they leave them uneaten, waiting for the freeze and thaw cycles of winter to produce a fermented feast for their spring bacchanal.

As northers blow and temperatures drop to startling depths, Burford holly berries turn black; sometimes even the yaupon's are ruined. But, the possumhaw fruits are still bright. This makes it a boon to gardeners looking for winter color.

If you live in Zones 6b to 9, and you'd like to plant a possumhaw in your garden, make sure you get a female tree; females have all of the fruit. Males aren't supposed to have any, although every so often you'll find one with a few berries. Don't be misled. Select your possumhaw in late fall. That's the time of year when the berries are fully out and in good color, and you'll know exactly what you're getting.

Then, choose a sunny site that is easily visible from the house or the driveway. Those gaudy red berries glowing all over the tree make a heartwarming sight on a gray winter day. And, they are a welcome sight to waxwings heading north in March.

Fast Food Stops
for Hummingbirds

Fall is the time of year when hummingbirds start heading south, flying close to the ground at speeds of up to sixty miles per hour. Hummingbirds are voracious feeders and fly low because they need to refuel their tiny bodies so often.

How voracious are they? Well, one study I read is extremely vivid. It compared the calorie consumption of an average-sized man—around 3,500 calories a day—to a hypothetical hummingbird of the *same* size, which would require 155,000 calories a day! Another way to look at it is, if you gave the man the same metabolism as the hummingbird, he'd have to eat 370 pounds of boiled potatoes each day to keep going. It's no wonder hummingbirds always have an eye peeled for snacks along the way. (Kind of like going on a trip with a car full of kids.)

People up north get to enjoy hummingbirds all spring and summer; those of us in the South and Southwest get to see them passing through, en route to and from their northern nesting grounds. By the end of September, they're usually getting ready to fly south on their annual fall migration to Mexico and Central America. And, instead of looking for golden arches along their route, they look for native flowers to provide them with a nutritious and delicious supply of nectar.

What they find, in many cases, are plastic feeders hanging from tree limbs and porch eaves, filled with brightly colored sugar water—junk food for hummingbirds.

When given the choice between sugar water and the sweet nectar of a fresh blooming flower—and I have friends who have experimented with this—a reasonably sane hummingbird will head for the nectar.

True, the energy value of sugar water is high. And, when you're flapping your wings at fifty to seventy-five flaps per second and darting all about, you need *lots* of energy. But a steady diet of sugar water robs hummingbirds of necessary trace minerals and vitamins found in nectar. Sugar water is fine as a backup (use only white sugar boiled in a five-to-one solution, keep the feeders clean, and leave out the dye), but a profusion of flowers is best.

The flowers that attract hummingbirds are all colorful, ranging from vivid reds to golden yellows to vibrant blues. The favored blooms tend to be tubular or trumpet-shaped. And, although a number of imported blooms, such as eucalyptus and orange trees, attract hummingbirds, native flowers are the big favorites. This is not surprising, because these are the flowers that hummingbirds have evolved with.

Turk's cap (*Malvaviscus arboreus* var. *Drummondii*), scarlet sage (*Salvia coccinea*), Gregg's salvia (*Salvia Greggii*), mealy blue sage (*Salvia farinacea*), penstemon sage (*Salvia penstemonoides*), trumpet vine (*Campsis radicans*), and a fall flowering of coral honeysuckle (*Lonicera sempervirens*) are hummingbird favorites in my garden.

Each of these handsome flowers or vines has many reasons for being an asset to a home landscape, but I'd plant them just for the pleasure of looking out the window and spotting hummingbirds every morning and afternoon from July to October.

They pause in midair while they stick their long, slender beaks into the flowers and suck out the nectar. Their body feathers are sleek and shiny, and the wings are beating so fast they are virtually invisible.

To make a hummingbird garden, choose a small area where the flowers will be massed very closely together. You will want to make a big splash of color so the hummingbirds can find you. Ideally, you'll want a full day of sun on your garden, although half a day is enough to get good blooms.

Put the Turk's cap where it will be in the most shade. This is a long-lived perennial that gets bush-sized each summer and dies down to the roots each winter after frost. The red flowers are like small, unopened hibiscus blossoms.

By a fence or old stump, but not right next to your house, plant the trumpet vine. This is the vigorous vine you see in alleys, holding up sagging garages. It thrives on sun and neglect (my kind of plant) and it can be aggressive. But, it is also gorgeous, with its shower of orange and yellow flowers.

The coral honeysuckle is quite well-mannered. It only needs a fence, trellis, or arbor to climb.

The salvias can be planted in any flower bed arrangement or in pots on a patio. You might also go with coral bean, which grows like Turk's cap.

The hummingbirds and I share a special affection for anisacanthus. This is actually a shrub, but it blooms so profusely that it fits perfectly into a flower garden. The dainty tubular flowers can be yellow, pumpkin, deep orange, or scarlet.

Anisacanthus can be used as a single specimen shrub, in a mass planting, or as a pot plant on a sunny patio. There are five species of anisacanthus, all native to the Southwest. The most cold-hardy is flame acanthus (*Anisacanthus quadrifidus* var. *wrightii*), which will tolerate 15°F if its roots are kept fairly dry.

By the way, I heartily recommend Mathew Tekulsky's *The Hummingbird Garden* (Crown Publishers, Inc.). It's everything you've ever wanted to know about hummingbirds—and a lot you *didn't* know you wanted to know. This illustrated book is devoted entirely to the many fascinating and beautiful varieties of hummingbirds, how they live, how they behave, and how you can attract them to your property.

Goldenrod Is Nothing to Sneeze At

Depending on your point of view, if you come across a field of goldenrod (*Solidago*) waving gently in the fall breeze, you'll do one of two things: reach for your camera—or reach for a handkerchief!

Everyone knows goldenrod as "that blankety-blank plant that causes hayfever." Not true! This is a scurrilous, unfounded charge. Hayfever is caused by airborne pollens (not to mention airborne pollutants, but that's another soapbox).

Don't believe me? Okay, let's review some of that birds-and-bees stuff we all learned back in kindergarten: All flowers produce pollen to fertilize other flowers of the same species. A fertilized flower then produces seeds, and another generation is on its way.

Sex by long-distance is not all that easy, however, so flowering plants have devised a number of ways to bridge the gap. Air-pollination is the most ancient. The basic idea is to get so much pollen into the breezes that a sufficient quantity cannot fail to fall on flowers of the right sex and the right species. When you think about just how *much* pollen it takes to do the job, well, no wonder you get hayfever.

But, there's another way plants get pollinated. Bees, butterflies, and hummingbirds carry pollen. And, if you've ever watched them do it, you may have noticed that they generally head for the biggest, brightest, and sweetest-smelling blooms.

Examine the flower of a goldenrod closely. You'll find that there are actually hundreds of tiny flowers clustered together to make the very showy head. There is also a faint but pleasant fragrance. Now, do you hear a faint humming? That's the sound of bees. There might be several bees on each head of flowers. The bees are covered with pollen, and, as they fly from one flower to another, they are transferring pollen, thus fertilizing the flowers.

The point is, goldenrod is *bee*-pollinated, not wind-pollinated. So, when you start sneezing, look around for the real culprit: ragweed. Ragweed is wind-pollinated, has an insignificant bloom, and is very common in every way.

Ragweed (*Ambrosia*) can have large leaves on thick green stalks that tower over your head, or it can grow only about knee-high and have grayish, narrowly divided leaves. The tall ones are found in seasonally moist or shaded grounds. You will find the small ones where it is very rocky or dry. Sometimes the two kinds can be seen growing just a few yards apart. They are most frequently found in disturbed ground that has been abused and prevented from developing its more civilized climax vegetation.

I often see the giant ragweed along creeks in the backyards of fancy suburban homes or in parks. There are many kinds of smaller ragweed, and they are usually found on bluffs and unmown vacant lots or in semiabandoned pastures.

Ragweed is an annual and very easy to pull out. Once you learn to recognize it, you can pull it up in the spring, long before it ever thinks about blooming. If you pull it up while the goldenrod is blossoming, you can prevent some seed from ripening and dropping to the ground to start next year's crop.

As for the goldenrod, I suggest that you just enjoy it out in that field. It's gorgeous, especially backlit by the setting sun. But, many wild goldenrods are a little too rambunctious to put in your garden. The one you are admiring might have a very invasive root system. In fact, that field we mentioned earlier might be just one plant!

The defense rests.

Trash Trees: Mother Nature's Band-Aids

Think of all the trash trees you wouldn't plant on a bet—the ones that get planted for you anyway by birds, wind, or squirrels. That list will include: Mimosa (*Albrizzia Julibrissin*), tree of heaven (*Ailanthus altissima*), Russian olive (*Elaeagnus angustifolius*), Chinese tallow (*Sapium sebiferum*), Chinaberry (*Melia azedarach*), Norway maple (*Acer platanoides*), and white mulberry (*Morus alba*)—all non-natives that have naturalized in various parts of the country. Add to the list natives such as silver maple (*Acer saccharinum*), boxelder (*Acer negundo*), and hackberry (*Celtis laevigata*).

These are the weeds of the tree world, growing so fast that their wood is weak. Most of them mature and die in about thirty years, and their last ten years of life are usually painful to watch. They generally look pretty messy most of the time, continually dropping litter and seeds. Naturally, these trees are as prolific as rabbits. Every seed seems to sprout, and every sprout seems to live. And they're happy just about anywhere; no soil is too compacted, too wet, or too sunny. They'd really love to put down roots in your yard.

You can look at it two ways: These trash trees are either very adaptable or they have very low standards.

Why did Mother Nature give us trash trees? Because without them, many trees of higher quality couldn't get established. This is how it works: Nature, as we learned in high school physics, abhors a vacuum. So, when a flood, landslide, or tornado has wrecked all of the existing vegetation and the soil is in danger of erosion, these spring-up-anywhere trash trees, along with weeds of the rankest description, become botanical "band-aids."

Their roots hold the soil, and their droppings become humus, giving better quality plants a chance to get established. Their thirty-year lifespan is the right amount of time to get a woodland going again. By the time the trash trees begin to die, young shade trees are outgrowing them, understory trees are producing fruit, groundcovers are able to find enough leaf mulch to gain a foothold, and a fledgling woods is beginning to provide habitat for a rich array of plants and animals.

The trouble is that, years ago, way back before we got so smart, we actually imported trash trees from all over the world. They were highly touted by garden writers (we don't always know what we're talking about!), promoted and sold by nurseries, enthusiastically bought by home owners, and planted everywhere.

Here in Texas, we are continuing this cycle with Chinese tallow. You don't have to look very hard to find people who will tell you how wonderful this tree is: healthy, fast-growing, and hard to kill, even in the hands of developers and first-time, inexperienced homeowners. It has great red fall color, even in environments too warm for most trees to color. The white fruits of the female are decorative all winter and attract birds. Sounds like a winner, right?

Not according to what we're hearing from environmentalists, bird watchers, and botanists: Chinese tallow is an environmental disaster. Like the beautiful but infamous flower *Lythrum salicaria* in the Northeast and several species of tamarix in the West, Chinese tallow is overrunning our wetlands. It is choking out the native vegetation that supports our wildlife. Wherever cuts are made for roadwork, an area is cleared for utility lines, or a hurricane destroys vegetation along the bayous near Houston, Chinese tallow rushes in to fill the void.

When this happens in China, the results are just as Mother Nature intended. Here, however, it's the wrong band-aid. Whatever insect, fungus, or rodent that might feed on tallow seedlings to keep them under control in China doesn't live here. And we certainly wouldn't want to import them; that kind of response more often than not just creates new environmental headaches. Nutria and walking catfish are examples that come instantly to mind. Here, the tallows establish themselves too thickly, and the oaks, maples, sweetgums, wax myrtles, and other native vegetation that should be populating our wetlands can't get a toehold. They get squeezed out because they are operating within the natural limits of their environment, programmed to prevent a population explosion; the tallow, however, is operating *without* its natural brakes.

Leslie Sauer, landscape architect and environmental restorationist of Andropogon Associates in Philadelphia, recommends that Norway maple and other noxious species be banned from being planted in the Northeast. The maple releases a toxic substance into the soil that prevents other plants from growing. She told me of one place in the Northeast where the land was cleared to make way for a new road. Four years later, Norway and sycamore maples (another imported trash tree) were well established and had kept some *three hundred* native species from returning.

I am sure that in fifty thousand years nature would get this all sorted out. But, if we don't intervene right now, Chinese tallow, Norway maple, and other imported trash trees will significantly reduce the numbers of many of our native species—both plants and animals—and none of us really knows how far the domino effect will reach.

Jean Michel Cousteau gave a talk in which he spoke about the dangers of lost species. He made a wonderful analogy: A plane is flying along with a madman on board. The madman is taking out rivets and tossing them away. The plane continues to fly along until, inevitably, one rivet too many is removed . . . and the plane comes apart. Our earth resembles that plane. The rivets are our many animal and plant species, all mysteriously and marvelously working in harmony to keep us aloft.

We are losing rivets all over the United States, and alien trash trees are one reason why. Last summer, when my husband and I were driving from Connecticut to Tennessee, we were horrified by the amount of ailanthus deserts we saw—miles and miles of highway, lined with thickets of nothing but ailanthus. Woodlands of native oak, maple, and tulip poplar were sometimes seeding out right over them, but no seeds were able to penetrate down to the soil through those blankets of ailanthus. Not even smooth sumac (*Rhus glabra*), one of our most vigorous suckering native shrubs, a band-aid plant of the first order, was able to penetrate.

If we're going to save our natural heritage of native species, we're simply going to have to help out. If we want to turn raw, abused land back into a native, self-functioning woodland, it's going to be necessary for individuals, as well as environmentally oriented groups such as native plant societies, Boy and Girl Scout troops, and garden clubs, to step in and do some of Mother Nature's work for her.

First, get rid of those exotic trash trees. You don't have to use poisons to do it; some can be easily cut down. Others will sprout again, so you'll need to remove them by the roots. It's possible to uproot trees as large as six inches in caliper with an iron bar and a little muscle power.

Then, plant very small, container-grown oaks, elms, and understory trees in late fall, or while they are dormant in the winter. It's important to plant these trees in the right combinations and at the appropriate spacings. Observing uninvaded woodland of the same habitat near you is the best way to do this. Essentially, you've got to count species and try to duplicate the composition and spacing the best way you can. Then, gather up all of your neighbors' bagged leaves to use as mulch, and use burlap to control erosion, if necessary.

Then, we have to hope that enough pieces of nature are still around to fill in the blanks. Because, the blunt truth of it is, as technologically sophisticated as we are, we are no more capable of completely reconstructing a simple, natural habitat than we are of building a human body from scratch.

Creating Habitats

People are so naive about plants, Ellie thought. They just chose plants for appearance, as they would choose a picture for the wall. It never occurred to them that plants were actually living things, busily performing all the living functions of respiration, ingestion, excretion, reproduction—and defense.

People who imagined that life on earth consisted of animals moving against a green background seriously misunderstood what they were seeing. That green background was busily alive. Plants grew, moved, twisted, and turned, fighting for the sun; and they interacted continuously with animals—discouraging some with bark and thorns; poisoning others; and feeding still others to advance their own reproduction, to spread their pollen and seeds. It was a complex, dynamic process which she never ceased to find fascinating. And which she knew most people simply didn't understand.

MICHAEL
CRICHTON
Jurassic Park

Little Bluestem
Schizachyrium scoparium

How Natural Is Natural?

There is much talk these days about natural land-scapes, a subject especially close to my heart. A natural landscape, just so we're all on the same wavelength, is the antithesis of the controlled environment found in a typical suburban yard. You know the kind—the one with the perfect lawn unmarred by weed or leaf, the rigid fringe of hedge that never peeps above a window sill, the scentless, overbred flowers lined up in neat rows, and the tree pruned within an inch of its life.

I have two books on the subject, and after reading them, I realized that the phrase "natural landscape" is open to some interpretation. Ken Druse's *The Natural Garden* and Jeff Cox's *Landscaping with Nature* both give directions on how to create woodland and grass gardens and how to arrange a rocky stream to look like Mother Nature made it. So far, so good.

The illustrations in these books, however, tell a different story; these "slices of nature" are inhabited by plants from all over the world. And, while a few of them are able to sustain themselves, most would die without human intervention. In his text, Cox mentions hundreds of natives in natural combinations, but then you get to the plans. They call for the usual nursery selections, and that means, for the most part, ill-adapted aliens.

I belong to the school that believes a natural landscape should be composed of only those plants that would have *naturally* occurred on that site. That means native plants—combined in the way that Mother Nature arranges them.

Today, many native plant lovers and environmentalists are taking this innovative and, to me, quite sensible point of view.

When you think about it, this perspective has a lot of merit. For one thing, it's an extremely low-maintenance approach; the only water the plants need comes from normal rainfall (after being established, of course). One plant doesn't get in another's way because millennia have taught them how to grow together harmoniously. And, of course, there's the welcome bonus of small wildlife, such as butterflies, anoles, and fireflies, who add beauty and interest to the scene. This wildlife is not nearly as fond of imports.

"Natural" in its purest sense—how Mother Nature managed things before we started helping her out—just doesn't exist in North America anymore, with the exception of Alaska and parts of Canada. Nature's management tools included vast herds of grazing animals and prairie and forest fires that might cover hundreds of square miles. Both were natural controls for the environment, and both are, of course, long gone. Even floods have been mitigated.

Obviously, there's just no way for us to return our country to the way it used to be when Native Americans were the stewards. We're not going to give up our farms, highways, factories, and shopping centers—especially our shopping centers. And we certainly don't expect our population to reduce itself to the number of people who lived here when Columbus dropped anchor.

But, we *can* act to save what precious wilderness we still have. Europe has pretty much destroyed theirs. We, in the Americas, have a chance to do better. All we need is some foresight, self-restraint, and common sense.

We can do something else, too. We can recreate our natural habitats in parklands, along highways, on the grounds of schools and businesses, and around our homes. They won't be *true* natural habitats, of course. In the strictest sense, recreating a true natural habitat may not be possible, even in our vast national parks. Yellowstone, however, is making a valiant attempt; it's trying to build up a herd of buffalo and reintroduce natural predators. It will be interesting to see how it all works out.

But those of us who own a bit of land—and you really don't need acres and acres—can have a modified natural native landscape. An area no larger than a typical suburban lot is enough to recreate a miniprairie or woodland around your home.

Many people are astounded to hear that they can have a miniwoodland on their property. But, they'd probably agree that they have enough land to accommodate two, three, or four shade trees, along with a complement of understory trees and assorted native shrubs, vines, groundcovers, and wildflowers. Well, that *is* a woodland.

A prairie landscape is perhaps harder to imagine. You are probably picturing crumpled stalks of brown grass and maybe a scraggly tree. Let me assure you that this is not what you would be attempting to achieve. I've seen lovely prairie home landscapes that have an arc of tall prairie grasses, thick and lushly green in the summer, golden with a tawny color in the winter, and dancing with wildflowers in the spring. You can mow walkways through the tall grasses to reach open spaces such as lawns, patios, or decks. For trees and shrubs, use the ones that were found along local creeks that once naturally bordered the prairies. This combination of woodland and grassland is called a verge, and it is the richest habitat of all. Flowers, fruits, and wildlife abound.

As for maintenance, if your grass is not being grazed by buffalo, land tortoises, or rabbits, you will have to mow occasionally. If you don't have deer, elk, or moose to browse your shrubs and trees, you'll have to prune once a year. And, every once in a while, you'll either have to have a real fire (it's possible to have a "cool burn" with firemen beside you), or you'll have to cut down saplings and brush that would have been burned, removing thatch or dead wood that hasn't decomposed enough.

The truth of it is, wherever you live in the United States, there is a gorgeous natural habitat that you can recreate. The rocky diversity of Idaho's grasslands or the Mojave Desert could make a landscape worthy of being featured in any home and garden magazine. There is simply no end to the natural landscapes that America has to offer.

In order to maintain this precious natural history, we as gardeners can make a big difference. We can use our native plants in natural combinations, cleaned up just enough to suit our aesthetic tastes or to keep our fussy neighbors happy. In doing so, we do more than give ourselves an attractive, easy-care landscape. We help preserve our plants, their gene pools, and at least some of the animals that evolved along with them.

Create Your
Own Woods

One of the smartest things I ever did was to select a mother who owns a good-sized piece of unspoiled woodland in east Texas. My escapes to that serene haven of arboreal beauty and welcome quiet are far too infrequent.

Although, to be truthful, things aren't all that quiet there. Bluebirds call to each other and play among the branches. Rustling leaves reveal the presence of quail searching for food. And there's almost always a breeze—and a squirrel or two—stirring in the treetops.

The woods are alive!

The bustle of our man-made world is shut out. You sit motionless in the woods on some moss, under a friendly old tree, and feel like you are a million and one miles away from traffic snarls, shopping malls, newscasts, and junk mail.

The lure of the woods is strong; people will drive hundreds of miles to camp or picnic out in the wild. Nearly everyone would like to have a home nestled in such a setting. Many are even willing to pay extra to buy a homesite with lots of mature trees on or at least abutting it.

But, many others live in suburban "bedroom" communities, where developers have scraped and leveled, planted a few puny shrubs, sprinkled grass seed, and called it landscaping. How dull!

Surely a woods is out of the question for this kind of setting . . . Or is it?

I'm happy to report that you can undo that 1950s look the developers saddled you with. Virtually any home, as long as it's on land that can support trees, can have a more natural, woodsy landscape. And, if you can't, or aren't, willing to give up the football field out front where Daddy and Junior play catch, then you can at least have a woodland in just a corner. Or, in your backyard.

Aside from obvious aesthetic appeal, there are many advantages to a woodland landscape. You don't have to water or fertilize. There is no need for you to even own a lawnmower or hedge clippers. Maintenance becomes annual instead of weekly, and it consists of a once-a-year project that includes pruning, cleaning out deadwood, maintaining paths, and fighting the undesirables: poison ivy, to which some people are highly allergic (like me); greenbriar, which creates thorny impenetrable thickets; Japanese honeysuckle, which is evergreen and smells good when in bloom, but is—how can I put this tactfully?—overly enthusiastic; or whatever is rampant and unwelcome in your region. The battle against such plants is an on-going engagement, because birds love their berries and replant the seeds on a regular basis. Furthermore, the roots are formidable: they laugh at ordinary applications of poisons, assuming you'd be so environmentally incorrect as to use them. Control is more realistic than eradication.

In the spring, before the leaves come out, the woods will seem to float in dainty white and pink. In the summer, the foliage is thick and lush, making your neighbors often invisible. Traffic noises are softened. It's even cooler inside your wooded sanctuary; the drop in temperature as you enter your woods is dramatic. Consider how that will affect your air conditioning bills.

In the fall, there is another burst of color, red and gold this time, made more vivid by evergreens. Don't rake the leaves. As they turn brown, they will protect the little woods violets and other flowers and provide the fertilizer for next year's round of beauty.

In the winter, the woods are sleeping. But the woodland creatures are not. If you have a lot of berries and seeds, your woods will be raucous and colorful with birds wintering over.

One of my favorite woodland gardens is in Bedford, Texas, a community midway between Dallas and Fort Worth.

The whole front yard is a post oak woods with a sprinkling of American elm, native red mulberry, cedar elm, and blackjack oak. The groundcover is Virginia creeper. Maintenance consists of keeping the Virginia creeper trimmed off of the trunks of the trees and cutting out unwanted saplings. One or two work days a year is more than sufficient. This beautiful woods is owned by a *lawnmower salesman!* Honest.

When he and his wife bought the lot, it was just one of many in a whole block of wooded lots. That's what they told me, but there was no evidence of woods by the time I saw it. All of the adjoining lots had been leveled by developers or owners. The new neighbors then put in St. Augustine or fescue lawns, which roll up to a line of foundation shrubs, and a sapling or two, which in twenty years will reach the size of the trees that were cut down. They must mow their lawns every week during the summer. (One can at least hope that these neighbors bought their lawnmowers from our salesman.)

Another post oak woodland garden I know is even more spectacular because it is more mature. Instead of many young post oaks six to nine inches in caliper and an average of ten feet apart, it has fewer, larger post oaks and a rich understory of fledgling post oaks, Mexican plum, redbud, rusty blackhaw viburnum, and native hawthorn. What a fairyland of white and pink in the spring! The owners have several acres, and so do each of their neighbors. The idea was to live in the woods, seemingly isolated from the rest of the world, while still being less than ten minutes from the nearest supermarket.

Unfortunately, the neighbors here are gradually cutting down their woods and laying out acres of St. Augustine sod, encircling it with chainlink, and then planting hundreds of red tip photinia by the fence to regain the privacy they purposely removed. Whenever I give a talk and mention these stories, the reaction from the audience is always the same: gasps of disbelief.

A cedar woodland I know has fared better because it backs up to parkland. Huge eastern red cedars, fifty feet tall with smooth straight trunks fourteen to sixteen inches in caliper form the canopy of this garden. Underneath are Carolina buckthorn and baby chinquapin oaks, both with delicately spreading branches and large shiny leaves. Scattered shrubs of American beautyberry are loaded with clusters of purple fruit in the fall. The groundcovers are naturalized evergreens—tall mondograss and vinca major. Birds flock to this garden. Last year, there was even a nesting pair of hummingbirds, which is rare for this part of Texas.

Well, now that I have all of you absolutely panting for at least one part of your property to be a woods, let me tell you how to make it that way. True, it won't resemble Sherwood Forest, but all of the basic components will be there for shade, beauty, and wildlife.

First, for those of you fortunate enough to already have a woods on your land, you can enhance its beauty by adding the color of small flowering trees and groundcovers native to your immediate area. Just be sure the spot you pick out for the new plant's home is similar to where it grows naturally.

If there are open spaces in your woods, plant your additional color here. If your woods is already very thick, cut down a few saplings of your dominant species to create space enough for other varieties. Then, mark each open place with a stake. Sit in your favorite viewing spot and imagine a small flowering tree where each stake is planted. You'll probably have to rearrange the stakes several times before you are satisfied. This is much easier as a two-person job, with one to view and one to move the stakes.

After you have chosen which trees (shrubs, flowers, and so forth) to use, plant small ones so they can establish themselves easily without a lot of supplemental watering. Make notes on your calendar to check new plantings at two-week intervals during the summer. Check in the spring and fall as well if rainfall is below normal.

If you are on a developer's lot, scraped clean with no telling whose soil heaped on top, or an old established yard with no pizazz, here is how to start your woods from scratch:

For every one hundred square feet of woods (10′ × 10′), there is usually one large tree, four to twelve inches or more in diameter, four saplings, and seventeen shrubs or understory trees. This is a dense woods that will screen a view and show little or no ground. Do not plant this density. Restrain yourself to one one-inch diameter shade tree, two understory trees, and two groundcover items such as low shrubs, ferns, or flowers. These plants will either sucker or seed out, so by the time the shade tree is four inches in diameter, you will have a dense woods, or you can keep the saplings thinned out and have an open woods.

Do not plant anything in a straight line. Are you familiar with the trick of naturalizing bulbs? Take a sackful of bulbs, and toss them out on the ground. You plant them where they land. Plan your woods the same way, but on a vastly larger scale. Obviously, I don't expect you to fling trees and shrubs all over your yard, but you can throw bricks or stones.

Begin by dividing your yard into ten- by ten-foot squares. This can be done with stakes or garden hoses or, in bare dirt, by making a groove with a hoe. Then, toss one brick into each square. At each brick, flag the spot for a shade tree and repeat the process for the flowering understory trees and for the groundcovers. If one of your shade tree bricks misses the intended square and ends up in another, don't throw it again. Plant the tree right there, and call it kismet.

If you need to create a visual barrier, plant evergreens or thicket-forming trees and shrubs in double strength on the offending boundaries.

Now you are ready to choose which plants to use. Notice, I said, *you*. There isn't room enough here for me to lay out the almost endless possibilities for each of you. Each area of the country has its own unique native woodland: pineywoods, post oak woods, maple oak woods, live oak woods, Douglas fir-aspen woods, mesquite woods, and scrub oak woods, to name a few. Each also has its own palette of complementary understory trees and shrubs.

So you, dear reader, will have to do a little research among your own local native plant experts. There's very likely a native plant society in your state (at least 33 states have one) or a wildflower society. Or, you may be fortunate enough to have a local nursery where they know and carry native plants.

However you arrive at your own woodland plant list, be assured that it will work with the basic scheme I've outlined. But, you must make sure you are planning the correct woodland habitat for your site, or you lose all of those easy-care benefits.

A woodland is a year-round visual treat. In the summer, it is green and cool. In the spring, there are the lovely limes and peaches of budding leaves, and the white, pink, and blue blossoms of the understory trees and woodland wildflowers. In autumn, there is colorful fall foliage and ripe berries, and often red and yellow flowers. In winter, the majesty of the trunks soaring to the sky, the tracery of the branches (often red or purple with the promise of life held in check), and the thick carpet of decomposing leaves hold the scene in hushed suspense.

Of course, what's all that compared to a lawn and a box hedge?

Little Prairie
by the House

When you hear the word "prairie," you probably picture a vast, seemingly limitless sea of tawny grass undulating to the horizon. There's not a single tree to be seen anywhere. Big sky country.

If you've ever read true-life stories of the pioneers, diaries and other first-person accounts, you know that the sound of the wind blowing through the grass was so constant and so loud that some poor souls were literally driven mad by it. You also probably remember tales of settlers beating out rampaging prairie fires with wet blankets, hoping to save the house and barn, while wild animals thundered by them, fleeing before the flames. And you remember the arctic-like blizzards from the "Little House on the Prairie" books and television series.

Is this what you can expect if you decide to recreate a prairie on your property? Relax. Unless your land measures in thousands of acres, those scenes I have just related are highly unlikely. Having a patch of prairie in your front yard is really not an off-the-wall idea. In its most basic sense, a prairie is just a tall lawn.

Our great western grasslands ended up being called prairies because the first Europeans to see them were French explorers who had come up the Mississippi River. "Prairie" is a

French word that means "meadow," although it may be hard for us to equate the two terms. Settlers in New England called their grasslands meadows, and proceeded to tame them with fences. When our forebears ventured out west and saw those staggering stretches of grassland, it never occurred to them to call them meadows; it would have been like calling a whale a guppy. So, they conveniently forgot that the French word meant the same thing and adopted prairie into our vocabulary.

In broad stroke, all native landscapes are divided into grasslands and woodlands. Grasslands can be wet or dry. In poorly drained areas, they are called marshes. On uplands, they are known as prairies or meadows. Although, to get you thoroughly confused, I must tell you that many people in the South call marshes prairies as well. In this book, whenever I use the term prairie I mean grasslands of all sorts, as Mother Nature maintained them before we imported invasive species.

The most exciting landscapes in North America (it's different in the tropics) are found where grassland and woodland meet. This border, the verge, is where the greatest number of plant species are gathered. The verge is where you will find the variety, the color, and lots of wildlife. That's where the action is.

Deep in a climax woods, a woods that is mature and able to sustain itself indefinitely, there is such dense shade that only a few plant species are adapted to live there; most species need sunshine if they are going to flower and fruit. Old-growth forests are important sanctuaries for many mushrooms and other specialized plants and animals that cannot thrive in less stable environments. Climax woodland, however, doesn't feed as many critters as the verge does.

A climax prairie is much the same. Thatch becomes so thick that no soil is available for seedlings. Plants can spread only by their formidable root systems. The longest-lived species are the only survivors. The flowers (called forbs) and most species of grasses are crowded out by the few climax grasses. These rarely flower or make seed. Bees, butterflies, birds, and small mammals are no longer able to find plenty to eat.

Climax prairies and forests are beautiful and peaceful. Scientists are observing that a patchwork of climax and verge is necessary to keep all species alive. But, climax landscapes take a minimum of a hundred years to develop. If you have the great luck to own a climax habitat, cherish it. But if you are going to be building a habitat from scratch, start with a verge.

We humans seem to have two elemental drives that influence where we choose to live. We want homes that are sheltered by trees—perhaps a trait held over from our arboreal ancestors. We also have a need to surround ourselves with open spaces where it is safe to walk, where lions and tigers and bears can't sneak up on us.

We can accommodate both basic needs with a successful and satisfying prairie garden that combines trees and shrubs from the verge with a mowed area for a lawn or walkway. How your particular prairie looks will depend on where you live, what you plant there, and how you maintain it. Choosing plants that can grow on your site naturally, without any help from you, is the key to success. For the most part, you want to choose the grasses that would have been climax for your site. Not only will they be dependable and long-lived, but they are invariably among the prettiest, the best behaved, and the most nutritious for wildlife.

Prairies vary considerably from east to west and according to the soil they live on. Most grasses prefer rich deep soil with a more alkaline pH. It's always interesting to drive north on the Natchez Trace Parkway in Mississippi; you pass a cypress swamp and immensely tall woods of sweetgum and oaks, with hydrangeas beneath—and then, all of a sudden, the trees become squat, and fields of grass and crops appear. What is happening here? The soil changes from acid sand to black clay loam, and just that quick you are out of the woods and onto the prairie.

This was prairie where the Chickasaw lived. Here the soil is rich enough to grow corn and other crops. There was once good forage for deer and elk here, with plenty of open space for bow-and-arrow hunting.

From early settlers' accounts, it seems that Long Island and the whole state of Rhode Island were once similar prairies. These eastern prairies are less than waist high and are, essentially, islands in an ocean of forest.

Broomsedge (*Andropogon virginicus*) is usually the most common grass. Plant it with a vetch or clover and as many of these flowers as you can, choosing local stock—fleabane (*Erigeron*), black-eyed Susan (*Rudbeckia*), milkweed (*Asclepius*), beebalm (*Monarda*), coneflower (*Echinacea*), and Joe-pye weed (*Eupatorium*). This mixture will get you started; you can add and refine as you go along.

In the Midwest, tallgrass prairies (often as tall as a man) were the dominant vegetation; trees were confined to the creeks. It feels especially appropriate to talk about these prairies in the past tense—they have almost disappeared. This land that grew lush grasses also grew lush crops (after all, corn and wheat are grasses, too), and very few prairie remnants were kept as hay meadows. Big bluestem (*Andropogon gerardii*), little bluestem (*Andropogon scoparius* or *Schizachyrium scoparius*), Indian grass (*Sorghastrum mutans*), and switchgrass (*Panicum virgatum*) are known as the "big four" of tallgrass prairie. These are the long-lived equivalents of oaks in a forest—the climax species, and they are a visual pleasure all year round. The fall and winter colors range from copper to gold; in the winter, the colors fade a bit but are still striking. Summer greens are rich and often bluish. Use switchgrass in the wetter sites and little bluestem where it is dry.

There are a myriad of other grass species, many quite lovely, as well as an overwhelming number of prairie perennials. One tiny prairie remnant in Waco, Texas, surrounded by city, was found to contain 20 species of grasses and 115 species of forbs. Twelve of these forbs are legumes (pea family), which are important nitrogen-fixers for the soil.

To start a tallgrass prairie, plan to begin with the big four grasses, and add these durable fall-blooming perennials: goldenrod (*Solidago*), aster (*Aster*), sunflower (*Helianthus*), gayfeather (*Liatris*), ironweed (*Vernonia*), and rosinweed (*Silphium*).

Also, use at least two legumes. Prairie clover (*Petalostemum*), clover (*Trifolium*), Illinois bundleflower (*Desmanthus illinoensis*), and milkvetch (*Astragalus,* which includes locoweed) are some of the most attractive and widespread.

Be aware, as you design your garden, that these flowers and grasses, with the exception of little bluestem and gayfeather, have stout aggressive root systems that can be kept in bounds only by pavement or weekly mowing during the growing season.

As you go further onto the Great Plains, the big four continue, especially little bluestem. But where it is really hot and dry and rainfall averages ten to fifteen inches a year, the grasses get shorter and the flowers become even more numerous. This is where you start getting spectacular spring colors, because there is plenty of room for annuals. Buffalograss (*Buchloe dactyloides*) and blue grama (*Bouteloua gracilis*) are two of the most prevalent and desirable short grasses. Easy-to-purchase spring flowers include paintbrush (*Castilleja*), Indian blanket (*Gaillardia pulchella*), prairie verbena (*Verbena bipinnatifida*), penstemon (*Penstemon* spp.), and Tahoka daisy (*Machaeranthera tanacetifolia*).

In the desert grasslands that stretch from West Texas to Tucson, Arizona, a mixture of side oats grama (*Bouteloua curtipendula*), plains bristlegrass (*Setaria macrostachya*), plains lovegrass (*Eragrostis intermedia*), and blue grama combine nicely for a soft, mid-shin look. Wildflowers include Indian blanket, Tahoka daisy (sometimes called prairie aster), desert marigold (*Baileya multiradiata*), and phacelia (*Phacelia integrifolia* or *P. intermedia*).

West of the Rockies, the grasslands are broken up by mountain ranges; rainfall patterns differ significantly, creating a number of distinct prairies. The southern California prairies near Los Angeles and San Francisco—usually called the valley grasslands—are probably the best known. The original grasses have been overgrazed and replaced by exotic annual species that give the famous golden summer color. But to start a real prairie, plant waist-high needlegrasses (*Stipa pulchra* and *Stipa cernua*), and the once ubiquitous soft-textured bluegrass *Poa scabrella*. Where temperatures often soar above 100°F., use two melic grasses (*Melica californica* and *Melica imperfecta*) with the needlegrasses.

Like the annual grasses, these original perennial prairie grasses will be green only from late October to late April. There are spectacular flowers to go with these grasses. The California poppy (*Eschscholtzia californica*) turns the hillsides golden in late February or early March. By April, it is joined by mariposa lily (*Calochortus*), lupine (*Lupinus*), owlclover (*Orthocarpus*), blue dicks (*Brodiaea*), baby blue eyes (*Nemophila,* especially *N. menziesii*), and gilia (*Gilia*).

The prairies of the Northwest are basically divided into moist prairies on the western side of the Pacific coastal ranges and dry ones on the eastern side. The coastal prairies are dry and dormant in the summer in Northern California, but get considerably moister as you go north into Oregon. The most important grasses are the same. California oatgrass (*Dathonia californica*) is difficult from seed but essential. It is commercially available in bales. Blue wild rye (*Elymus glaucus*) tolerates some shade; use it where the prairie meets the shrubs and trees at the verge. Red or molate fescue (*Festuca rubra*), a weeping bunchgrass with reddish flowers, doesn't become a dominant in California, but is so lovely you'll want to use it anyway. These are cool weather grasses, green in the spring, dormant in the summer where there is drought and in the winter where cold is severe. On especially moist sites, use tufted hairgrass (*Deschampsia caespitosa*) with its great heads of flowers that turn from green to red to gold.

On drier prairies, Idaho fescue (*Festuca idahoensis*) is a dominant, both in the northern California coastal prairie and on the eastern prairies, where it is joined by bluebunch wheatgrass (*Agropyron spicatum*) and the slightly shade-tolerant prairie Junegrass (*Koeleria nitida* or *cristata*).

Flowers for all these northwest prairies include blue dicks (*Brodiaea*), blue-eyed grass (*Sisyrinchium*), mariposa lily (*Calochortus*), lupine (*Lupinus*), clarkia (*Clarkia*), Oregon sunshine (*Eriophyllum lanatum*), shooting star (*Dodecatheon*), rosy corn salad (*Plectritis*), the big-headed clover (*Trifolium macrocephalum*) and, in really wet places, camas (*Camassia*). Be sure to use local species for long-term results.

You might opt to maintain your prairie the way Mother Nature did; she used prairie fires as a necessary tool to keep brush and trees out, so they wouldn't grow up and shade out the grasses. Fire is also important to invigorate some of the grasses; there have been numerous studies showing that both big and little bluestem increase their numbers only after a fire. A controlled burn, even in a suburban lot is possible and can be beneficial—or not, depending on when it is done. A fire in late summer doesn't hurt spring wildflowers, but it isn't good for fall ones preparing to bloom. On the other hand, a fire in the spring is definitely a boon to fall wildflowers.

Mother Nature also relied on grazing elk, pronghorn, deer, and buffalo as management tools. Today, we have horses, cattle, and sheep. Horses feeding lightly on a prairie seem to produce a pretty look, while cattle and other livestock that are kept grazing in one area for over a month seem to be detrimental for everything. This information won't affect your suburban home prairie, of course; I suspect you'll probably use a lawnmower or a scythe instead. I did once, however, have a client who rented a goat for one week every year.

I hate to end on a negative note, but Mother Nature didn't have to weed out invasive species to start a prairie—there weren't any in those days. You will. Or else watch your efforts be overrun. Once your prairie is well-established and functioning as one harmonious, organic unit, it can keep the weeds out by itself—but it will take a few years.

A Kinder, Gentler Desert Garden

What's wrong with this picture?

The groundcover is gravel, or uniformly sized bits of colored rock, carefully kept clean and tidy with one of those outdoor vacuum cleaners or a leaf-blower. Often, rocks of different hues, ranging from battleship gray to coral, are separated from each other by concrete scalloped edging. (Allowing them to mingle would be tacky!) Sometimes, the gravel is dyed green . . . to simulate a lawn? Occasionally real creativity is called into play, and you may find a stream of baby blue pebbles meandering beneath a miniature pink wrought-iron bridge.

Residing next to drip irrigation heads are cacti of various kinds, along with yuccas and other spiny succulent desert flora. Some homeowners, newly arrived from up north, become smitten with this exotic flora, and venture out into the desert to collect their own plants. They then proceed to cram as many as they can onto their properties, creating a confused mish-mash of "arms," "tongues," spikes, and daggers. Or, they will go to the other extreme, placing a single plant here, another way over there, still another at the other end of the yard. Each is ringed with white-washed river rocks. There is no cohesion here, no sense of flow, no drama.

Underneath it all are impenetrable sheets of black plastic, holding down whatever "weeds" may be lurking below, preventing dirt or sand from getting into the pristine gravel, keeping rain off the soil.

If you live between El Paso and Los Angeles, you've seen these desert gardens. They are everywhere. And they have absolutely nothing to do with the real desert.

The most vivid way to see how dramatically different the real desert looks is to visit Frank Lloyd Wright's Taliesin West in Scottsdale, Arizona, a suburb of Phoenix. To reach Taliesin West, you must first drive through miles of middle-class and upscale subdivisions. Here, you'll see those cactus and gravel landscapes in boundless variety. You'll also see another style of landscaping: lavish green lawns surrounded by luxuriant tropical plants. This, needless to say, gets watered once or twice a day. The cactus/gravel style, at least, makes a concession to the climate and water shortages. But both are as inappropriate as giggling during High Mass.

Ah, but then you enter the road that takes you up to Taliesin West, and the true desert surrounds you. This scene is far greener and softer than the gravel garden. The saguaros and yuccas are sensibly spaced apart, so that each can lay out a wide network of surface roots to catch even the merest hint of rainfall . . . sometimes as little as .01 of an inch! They are the trees of the true desert landscape.

The groundcover is not gravel. While there is bare soil and rock showing on the desert floor, it is more than half covered with a variety of soft, non-spiny plants that pull the whole scene together. They produce flowers after spring rains, feed numerous animals, and are an essential ingredient of this beautiful natural area.

Now here's the odd thing: Until recently, these lovely plants had been largely ignored by desert gardeners. If you live in one of the warm desert regions of this country, it's high time you became acquainted with these plants.

The most important groundcover plants for the warm deserts, such as the low altitude deserts in New Mexico, Arizona, and California, are two drought-deciduous shrubs called bur sage (*Ambrosia dumosa* and *Ambrosia deltoidea*). Thornless and gray-green in color, these knee-high shrubs are, like all groundcovers, vital as a unifying element in the landscape. I've seen no study on this, but I'd be willing to bet that bur sage is extremely important to many desert creatures. I can't believe that Mother Nature would produce so much of it if it weren't doing anybody any good.

Another thornless and soft-textured plant that is important to the true desert garden is brittle bush (*Encelia farinosa*). This evergreen shrub is blue-green in color and can get waist-high if it receives extra runoff. It possesses fairly large leaves for the desert and, in March, is covered with big yellow daisies—they can hang around longer if it gets some rain. Brittle bush looks especially good matched with another dependable desert flower, the globe mallow (*Sphaeralcea ambigua*). This perennial blooms for a long time and has satiny blossoms in orange or pink.

Small-leaved shrubs and trees such as creosote and palo verde soften the scene, making it prettier and more friendly to humans. Creosote (*Larrea tridentata*), a large evergreen shrub with tiny dark green leaves and bright yellow flowers, produces that wonderful after-the-rain scent the desert is famous for.

Palo verde (*Parkinsonia spp.*) is especially lovely up next to a smooth wall, where its lime-green trunks and branches show to best advantage. About twenty feet tall and wide, its finely textured foliage delivers a lovely soft look, and when the whole tree turns orange-gold with spring flowers it is nothing short of spectacular.

Most people are amazed to learn that grasses occur in the desert. They grow in clumps, but not close enough together to make a sod. You may be accustomed to thinking of grasses only in the context of a lawn, but in a desert garden they make marvelous accents and backdrops.

There is a surprising diversity of native desert grasses that once supported land tortoises, pronghorns, and other desert grazing animals. Sacaton (*Sporobolus wrightii*) used to be thick wherever the desert rivers flooded. Curly mesquite grass (*Hilaria belangeri*) grows at the base of saguaros, those wonderful giant cacti peculiar to the Sonoran Desert surrounding Phoenix and stretching west into California.

Purple three awn (*Aristida purpurea*) is one of the few native grasses readily available commercially for the low, hot deserts. When massed and in bloom, purple three awn looks like a low pink cloud hovering over the ground. For long-term results, it is best to use one of the desert climax grasses, even though they will be hard to find. Here are three good ones: In true desert sand, plant golden knee-high drifts of the bunch

A Desert Garden

grass, big galleta (*Hilaria rigida*). For a very different feel, use bush muhly (*Muhlenbergia porteri*); its foot-tall wavy stems make it look like it just has a permanent. Black grama (*Bouteloua eriopoda*) is more like a groundcover; it forms a wooly-white curly mat that is usually only about six inches tall.

By now, I hope you're creating a lovely desert landscape in your mind's eye: majestic cacti and dramatic yuccas, softened with bur sage, flowers, grasses, and lacy-leaved trees. . . . It provides a year-round color scheme of gray-green, blue-green, dark green, and lime-green with tawny grasses and bursts of vivid colors when the desert flowers bloom in the spring.

Drip irrigation goes with that traditional isolated-plant look I mentioned earlier; it doesn't work with the new and more natural desert look I've just described. Here a bubbler makes more sense. And not watering at all (once the plants have been established by watering with a hose for one to three years) makes even more sense. But that means you have to utilize every little drop of rain that falls on your land. Obviously, black plastic is a no no; it doesn't allow the rain to soak into the ground. To keep whatever rain falls on your property, use swales. Catch the run-off from the roof, the patio, and any paved walks or driveways. This captured water can easily double the moisture your plants would otherwise get.

Many landscape architects and designers in the Phoenix area are using something called the "envelope" approach. With this system, your house and the planting areas directly adjacent to the front door and in the courtyard get irrigated in a conventional manner. Here you can keep the indigenous desert plants looking fresher all year, and you can experiment with flowers such as cenizo from other desert regions. You can even keep a few beloved water-guzzlers alive. But outside the envelope, you allow Mother Nature to tend your landscape. There is the true natural desert with all its beauty for you to just sit back and enjoy.

What's wrong with *this* picture? Not a thing!

Mother Nature's Winter Garden

Last November, Andy and I drove down to Houston to visit with friends over the Thanksgiving weekend. Now, when I'm on the road, I'm a passenger—never a driver, if I can help it. Interstate driving is as stimulating as a warm-oil massage; I'm always afraid I'll just nod off. But, as a passenger, I'm free to plant-watch, which is one of my favorite pastimes. By now, I've been down Interstate 45 so many times that I sometimes think I should already have every tree and shrub along the way memorized. "Hmm, that boxelder is looking a little peaked this fall . . ."

On this particular trip, I decided to mentally design a winter garden, using only what struck my eye as we drove. (This Dallas-to-Houston route pretty much reflects the same vegetation you'd see driving from Kansas to South Carolina, except for the flora in the Great Smoky Mountains.)

What I noticed immediately was the lovely winter colors of the grasses. My favorite combination was a soft-looking, shortly mown grass that resembled a carpet of the palest yellow fluff. (Picture the color of unsalted butter.) It was beautifully highlighted by sweeps of a taller grass colored a scrumptious russet-orange. (Imagine the heart of a baked sweet potato.) Yummy combination.

This rich orange grass was one of three bluestems. All

three achieve the beautiful sweet-potato color and remain vibrant throughout the winter until March or April. In low places, there is brushy bluestem (*Andropogon glomeratus*), with thick bushy heads. On sandy embankments, where the nutrient levels are low, you'd find split-beard bluestem (*Andropogon ternarius*), still glistening with white tufts of fluffy seed up and down the stems. Closer to Dallas, where the soil is rich and heavy, there was little bluestem (*Schizachyrium scoparium,* formerly called *Andropogon scoparium*).

There were other tall grasses that were a nice tawny gold. When you have such a warm palette of colors, they seem most lively when backed by a cool color. The blue sky worked great as this backdrop, but even more inviting were the evergreens. The dominant evergreens I saw as we headed to the coast were: juniper (Eastern red cedar, *Juniperus virginiana*), yaupon holly (*Ilex vomitoria*), live oak (*Quercus virginiana* X *fusiformis*), shortleaf pine (*Pinus echinata*), loblolly pine (*Pinus taeda*), cherry laurel (*Prunus caroliniana*), and wax myrtle (*Myrica cerifera*).

You will probably be surprised, as I was, to learn that the evergreen that gave the most depth and sparkle to the scene was the juniper. It had the richest, most alive green—an eager, thrusting texture that was dark with blue shadows and highlighted with gold. By comparison, the yaupons and oaks had a silvery flatness. The pines were just too tall to properly set off the grasses. They were also too sparsely needled and altogether not as satisfying as the junipers.

As I composed my winter garden, I wondered how an accent of red-berried possumhaw (*Ilex decidua*) would look in my gold and green color scheme. Obligingly, one leaned over a fence toward me. It looked great. So did a mother yaupon, with translucent red berries peeking out between the leaves.

Then, I tried to picture a purple-berried American beautyberry (*Callicarpa americana*) in my imaginary winter garden. I never saw one, but I did find a knee-high thicket of coralberry (*Symphoricarpus orbiculatus*). If you think of coral as an orange-red color, you need to repicture this. Whoever named coralberry was thinking of raspberry-colored coral instead. The purple tones were as satisfying as the red, and my color scheme seemed complete.

I noticed then how the red and purple tones were repeated with the twigs of thicket plum (*Prunus gracilis*) and river birch (*Betula nigra*). The willows echoed the orange of the bluestems. The silhouetted shapes of sweetgum balls and pine cones, the papery hanging ornaments of boxelder, and the dark red cornucopias of sumac added even more interest.

On the way home two days later, the sky was leaden and wooly white with a steady drizzle. Yet the plant colors gleamed just as warmly in this dismal light. Mother Nature definitely had aesthetics in mind, as well as more practical matters, when she planned *her* winter garden.

A Winter Garden

Looking for a Good Neighbor? Try a Creek.

With the possible exception of W. C. Fields, humans seem to have a natural affinity for water. Maybe it's because we spent the first nine months of our lives immersed in it. Maybe it's because we evolved from sea creatures umpteen million years ago, and the call to return home is programmed into our genes. Or, maybe it's because we're 90 percent water ourselves. Whatever the reason, we gladly pay premium prices for lakefront or oceanside property when an identical home on the same-sized lot a hundred feet inland could be bought for much less.

And, while they avoid water in bathtubs, kids gravitate toward it in creeks and streams; they know that that's where the action is. There are crawfish to hunt and dragonflies to chase and, of course, great walls and dams to be erected from whatever rocks may be found nearby.

Being near water seems to be essential for the good life. My own home is not actually on a lake. But, in the winter, if I stand on tip-toe and look out of my second-floor bathroom window, through the branches of the leafless trees, I can almost make it out. All I can tell you is that it makes a big difference to me to just know it's there.

My dream is to someday own a home on a creek (or "crik," depending on what part of the country you live in).

For me, it's even more desirable than living next to the ocean or by a lake; creeks are more low-key, more restful. Someone once defined a creek as a "river with low blood pressure."

Some of you lucky people already have that pleasure. If you do, you are also aware that living on a creek—especially a creek in a populated urban area—also has a few drawbacks. (This is not a perfect world, friends.)

Probably, the biggest disadvantage is trash. After each rain, it seems as if the contents of every trash bag in town has washed up on the banks of your creek. I wish I could offer a solution, but I can't even get my daughter to keep her room clean. I certainly don't have any ideas about converting our fellow citizens to less messy lives. The only thing to do is budget time and/or money to get the trash cleaned up.

Erosion is another problem. Creeks will just naturally erode; that's how the Grand Canyon happened. But, we're not talking about millions of years here, we're discussing the visible erosion that seems to occur overnight. It happens, generally, as a result of misguided efforts at water control. Some years ago, engineers noticed that parking lots and lawns were contributing a lot of run-off to normal creek flows, and this extra flow was causing flooding. They decided that they would have to get that water moving faster, and the fastest way to move a lot of water, they determined, was to clear the creeks of trees and tall grasses that tend to slow the water down. Some of you may have just bought (or built) a house on a creek that was denuded of vegetation; it's not a pretty sight.

The "experts" are now waking up to the fact that this causes the creeks to erode *too* quickly. Moreover, the soil washed out of them starts building up downstream in lakes and rivers, resulting in more frequent—and costly—dredging operations. See what happens when you mess with Mother Nature? We now know that it's more important to *slow* the water down so it has a chance to soak in and help replenish our groundwater supply.

Another problem: Creeks often run dry in the summer. In my part of the country, this is natural and unavoidable and something that we native Texans understand (although it tends to upset recent arrivals). What *is* new, and a bad sign of the times, is that spring-fed creeks are running dry because the springs themselves are drying up. This occurs because the groundwater that feeds them is not being replenished. Parking lots, streets, and lawns do not allow rain to soak into the ground. Sometimes the local water board even lets someone buy all of your groundwater for watering a golf course or running a factory.

Still another difficulty concerns ownership. With creeks, you often own only to the middle of the creek bed, and someone else owns the other half. As a result, your view of the creek includes the opposite bank, over which you have no control. If your neighbor is a talented and tasteful gardener, count yourself lucky. Your neighbor might be a connoisseur of junked autos, proudly displaying his collection of rusty and mangled auto carcasses right across from your sundeck.

Even with all of these problems, a creek is a wonderful thing to have on your land. It offers you the possibility of having a little bit of Eden in your own backyard. You can hear gurgling water at least part of the year, and you can hear birds chirping all year long. And, you can make all of these surroundings as wild or as tame as you choose.

Of course, it's actually the vegetation found along the creek that makes it pretty and attractive to wildlife. And, a woodland setting is, I think, most desirable. The trees and groundcovers that have grown up the banks and out of the water are the typical woodland plants for the area and will vary considerably from one part of the country to the next. The trees right along the banks, within one or two feet of the water, are almost universal: sycamores, cottonwoods, and willows are the most common, with bald cypress often found in swampy areas in the South.

Because life along a creek is only safe until the next flood, creek plants are different from other plants. They have aggressive, wide-ranging roots for holding tight to the bank and the bit of soil they occupy. The smaller plants sucker extensively, and any bit of root that is washed away is capable of making a new plant wherever it ends up downstream. The trees grow fast and die young. The trick is getting established quickly and being able to reestablish quickly. Longevity and high quality are not rewarded.

If your stream is denuded of trees, and you want to change this, look around. You'll probably find numerous seedlings. If you're lucky, you'll have a large amount of saplings, or adolescent seedlings. You won't need all of them, but quite a few might be useful. Mark them with flagging tape so you won't accidentally destroy them. Choose the ones that are tallest or best placed for your landscape scheme, and pull up the rest. Let some stay clumped together and leave plenty along the fastest eroding part of your creek, to help hold the bank. These will become your canopy or shade trees.

If you're impatient to gain some height in your landscape, you can buy bottomland trees native to your area to give you comfort for the first year. If you have more patience than money, don't worry, your landscape will grow much faster than you'd imagine, probably as fast as one containing purchased trees. Plus, by using what has established there naturally, you will have exactly the trees with the right genetic makeup for your creek.

Once you have an idea of where most of your trees will be located, plan your overall scheme. Can you dam to create a little pool of slower-moving water that can be maintained at a dependable height? (You'll need permission from the county to do this.) Can you get lots of sun to this spot for hibiscus and other water plants that require plenty of light? Or, will a totally wooded setting fit in best with your neighbors' landscapes? Do you need evergreen screening for one part, or do you have enough room for a more natural looking thicket of deciduous trees mixed with evergreens? Planning is easiest if you can draw your ideas on paper. See if you can find your land survey. This is often called a plat plan and is usually one of the pieces of paper you get (and pay for) when you buy your house. It shows your property lines, utility easements, the hundred-year flood line, and the exact position of your house on your property. Sometimes, it also shows the location of a few especially large trees. Check the scale. Most often, it is twenty feet to the inch but is sometimes sixty feet to the inch or some other number. Measure a few key boundaries to make sure your survey was done accurately. Then, have a couple of copies made.

Now, you're ready to draw. Block out where you want woods, where you want seating areas, paths, stairs, and so on. Plot your trees.

Imagine how the trees will look when they're all grown up. Then look at them from all of the most important windows in your house, as well as from any outside seating areas. If it is too hard to picture, have your friends stand outside and pretend to be trees. (Is this a theme party idea?)

Once you have the walking areas and the shade trees in place, you get to the really fun part. This happens when you plan the flowering trees and groundcovers that will make your creek area a special garden. Plant lots of understory trees with low shrubs or woodland flowers and ferns for ground-cover. For screening, plant thickets or evergreens. Remember, the actual plants you choose need to be appropriate for the creeks where you live. Here are some samples of what you might do:

In the Midwest, plant indigo bush (*Amorpha fruticosa*). If the water level is more dependable because of a dam, and you have plenty of sun, you could also plant buttonbush (*Cephalanthus occidentalis*). Both are bushes that can even-tually become very large shrubs or small trees. The amorpha has purple spikes in the spring. The buttonbush has fragrant white globes of flowers all summer that attract butterflies.

At the feet of these shrubs you could plant a groundcover of frogfruit (*Phyla* spp.), with cardinal flower (*Lobelia car-dinalis*) for red flowers in late summer. For white fall flowers and a rich winter color of cinnamon orange, plant a clump of brushy bluestem (*Andropogon glomeratus*), if it grows in your area. If not, try switchgrass (*Panicum virgatum*), with its feathery plumes and dark golden fall color. All of these plants like at least a half day of sun and are excellent for erosion control.

In the Southeast, creeks are deeply shaded. Plant bloom-ing understory trees on the banks with blue-flowered ruellia and amsonia beneath. At the muddy edge, have a groundcover of white-blooming lizard's tails, (*Saururus cernuus*) with chain fern (*Woodwardia areolata*) just barely up the bank and below a thicket of Virginia sweetspire (*Itea virginica*). Screen with evergreen yaupon holly (*Ilex vomitoria*).

Further north, use a thicket of silky dogwood (*Cornus amomum*) or red-stemmed dogwood (*Cornus sericea*) for erosion control. Evergreens may include inkberry holly (*Ilex glabra*) or bayberry (*Myrica pennsylvanica*).

Along the Gulf Coast, screen with wax myrtle (*Myrica cerifera*) and plant palmettos (*Sabal minor*) and scarlet sage (*Salvia coccinea*) under swamp haw (*Viburnum nudum*).

In the Southwest, you're definitely into arroyo, not creek, country. Desert willow (*Chilopsis linearis*) and other trees requiring good drainage, but grateful for the underground wa-ter and the shade cast by the arroyo banksides, grow along the arroyos with numerous wildflowers. These plants are often protected by river stones that prevent flood waters from un-earthing them.

For those of you with fully planted creeks where it would take a machete to get through to the water, your job is not planting, it's pruning. At first, cut out the invasive plants such as trash trees and Japanese honeysuckle. If you still can't reach the water, cut a narrow path by removing saplings of the dominant shade trees.

Observe your woods for a full year. Each time something blooms or fruits or otherwise proves itself worthy, tie a ribbon around it. If it has a ribbon, it becomes sacrosanct; everything else is a candidate for thinning out—unless, of course, you've grown to love the surprises and treats that Mother Nature provides in a dense woods. If so, just let her have her way with it while you sit back and enjoy.

Floating Bladderwort
Utricularia radiata

The Floating Bladderwort

That's a floating *what?*" my husband exclaimed.

"A floating bladderwort," I replied. "Or, to put it more scientifically, *Utricularia radiata.*" Instantly, floating bladderwort became Andy's favorite native plant—sight unseen, mind you!

Bladderwort makes a wonderful addition to a natural earthen water garden, the kind that can support life such as fish and microscopic animals. Think of the fun you can have when you introduce your friends to this plant. Then, watch their faces when you tell them it's a carnivore. Don't worry. It only eats microorganisms in the pond; your pet poodle will not be devoured if it roams too close to the edge.

Floating bladderwort is native from Nova Scotia all the way to the Gulf of Mexico. You'll find it in still water and slowly meandering streams, in areas where the soil is acid.

Its name is very descriptive. A wort is a small plant, in this case two or three inches wide. Each plant floats, buoyed up by tiny little bladders that grow at the end of its radiating arms. The roots trail down into the water and are normally anchored to other submerged water plants.

I observed several dozen bladderworts over a period of years in an East Texas lake. They always grew in exactly the same spot, leading me to wonder if, in fact, they were rooted in the shallow bottom. All of the books I'd read said differently, but I know how new books quote old books, and sometimes the wrong information gets passed along as gospel. (I once found that an error in one of *my* books got repeated a year or two later as a "fact" in someone else's book. That's scary!)

Either my observations were faulty, or those books were passing along bad information. So, in the interest of science, my husband and I donned face masks one fine spring day and spent a chilly hour submerged in that particular lake, trying to find the answer. The water was very murky, and even an underwater flashlight wasn't too much help. We kept losing the delicate roots in all of the other underwater flora.

I wish I could report that our dedication to truth-seeking was rewarded with the startling news that the books were wrong, and I had been right. No such luck. As far as we could tell, the bladderwort is *not* attached to the bottom. The books were right.

In spite of its comical name, bladderwort is quite pretty, with tiny yellow flowers (three to four per float) that bloom in the summer. It's an ideal size for a small pond, whereas water lilies and lotuses need to be potted to keep them from taking over. If your water garden contains fish, they'll find the floating bladderwort a nice source of food and shelter. You might even be surprised to see a migrating duck drop in one day for a quick snack.

Most folks who already have water gardens use clean tap water, which is too sterile to support microorganisms. These conventional ponds have artificial sides and a scoured bottom on which rests an ugly recirculating pump. All the mechanics show through the clear water. Small fish can live here, as long as the water has been allowed to sit so that the chlorine can dissipate. But you won't get the full self-supporting cycle of pond life.

In an earthen pond, there is mud in the bottom where fish can lay their eggs and where underwater plants can grow. The water is murky with the goop of life and camouflages what you don't want to see.

If you have a tap-water pond and would like to be a tad more adventurous, you can convert it to a natural, living, pond. It's relatively easy. Just go out and find a body of water that is rich in microorganisms. Then, scoop up a few buckets of this living scum, and add it to your conventional pond.

You can tell that the water is rich in this vital goop if the pond or roadside ditch has a murky look. You also need to add lots of submerged plants. It takes almost a year for all of the parts of the ecosystem to operate together well enough to support bladderworts.

Then, test the water to make sure it is quite acidic, definitely below six on the scale. It's best to have an earthen bottom; if you have a cement pond, you'll need to add three to four inches of mud.

One more thing—don't expect to buy bladderwort at your neighborhood nursery. You will have to find it yourself out in the wild, and bring it home in a bucket.

Lupinus texensis

Where Do We Go from Here?

The sun, the moon and the stars would have disappeared long ago, had they happened to be within reach of predatory human hands.

HAVELOCK ELLIS

I would argue that just the turning of our attention to the natural world tends to subvert our anthropocentric heritage. We may be on some sort of a halting journey toward understanding the world, and ourselves within it, as one system.

THOMAS J. LYON
This Incomperable Lande

The Eighth
Deadly Sin

〜

*I may be a native Texan, but I'm basically a city girl. So
it's a genuine treat for me to go out to a real working
ranch. I can be just as wide-eyed as any visitor from back
east—the big difference being that, instead of looking at
the cattle and horses, I look at the vegetation.*

For the past two years, I've been watching a rape in
progress. Until recently, when you looked out of my friend
Dorothy's ranch-house window, you were treated to a marvelous view of typical Texas Hill Country beauty.

That view is rapidly disappearing, and, by the time you
read this, it may well be almost gone. You see, one of her
neighbors became aware of the hefty tax breaks ranchers
receive for clearing the land and turning it into pasture.
Well, he's definitely clearing the land—he's doing it with a
bulldozer.

The bitter irony is that this land will never become pasture; the hills are too steep to grow grass, and the soil is too
thin. The main thing that *will* grow on this land is the juniper
that is being bulldozed away.

Our present tax laws do not encourage land conservation. Landowners are penalized for allowing land to lie fal-
low and regenerate itself. A rancher and his or her survivors
can never retire; the ranch must be worked to qualify for tax
breaks.

If they just want to sit on their backsides and sip cool
drinks in their golden years, they're going to have to pay
much higher, very likely unaffordable, taxes for the privilege.
Either that, or sell off the land that has probably been in their
family for generations, and move away to a condo.

Of course, ranching, even with subsidies, is no quick and

easy path to riches. We're all eating less red meat these days. Many ranches are being sold to wealthy urbanites who want to escape the frenetic city life and enjoy the beauty of the wide open spaces. These city slickers don't want to actually *be* ranchers, they just want to wear boots and hats. When faced with the choice of paying higher taxes or running a few head of cattle on their spread, they quickly opt for the cows.

Dorothy's neighbor will get his tax breaks. But at what a cost. Those once-lovely hills will look like a devastated wasteland for generations to come. Maybe forever. This land, like the desert, heals very slowly.

And you thought you had to go to the Brazilian rain forests to see how we mistreat Mother Nature.

There's another ranch out in Bosque (Bos-key) County, west of Waco, that I got to visit in my professional capacity of landscape designer. The owners hired me to come out, look around, tell them what was growing there, how they could preserve what needed preserving, get rid of what needed getting rid of, and draw up a landscape plan for around the main house. It was a treat for me, because I didn't see one single non-native plant on the entire spread.

So what? So this: It's very rare these days to see countryside that *is* all native. Weeds from Europe, Asia, and Africa are so widespread and prevalent that most people are amazed to learn that they don't actually belong there, that they are invaders. Believe it or not, the Deep South once existed without a trace of kudzu, and the Great Plains states were once free of Russian olive.

As I explored the Bosque County ranch, I didn't see a single Japanese honeysuckle smothering the live oaks and viburnums. There was no Johnson grass, Bermuda grass, or African bluestem grasses crowding out the feathery, delicately colored, gently waving meadow of native grama grasses with its sprinkling of little bluestem and flowers.

Yet, as beautiful as this rugged ranchland is, I couldn't help but reflect on how it has been shaped by civilization. It's very different from the native landscape the settlers first saw.

Until one hundred fifty years ago, when this land was "managed" by nature, there were mid-grass prairies, thick and glowing with little bluestem, big bluestem, and Indian grass. Only in the poorer soils that couldn't hold plenty of water and organic matter did the gramas and other short grasses grow. This particular pasture should have been mostly little bluestem. And, there would have been no patches of bare earth showing between the clumps of grass.

The soil itself is sadly depleted—ruined by European farming practices that are better suited to deeper soils and higher rainfalls. Pastures are fenced in, changing the feeding habits of cattle. Once, when cows grazed on open rangeland, they nibbled on their favorite bits of vegetation, then moved on in search of more. Fenced in, they are forced to eat what is available—and *only* what is there. The land is soon over-grazed to the point of desolation.

The woodlands still have oaks and viburnums and other long-lived trees and shrubs, but the shorter-lived redbud, Carolina buckthorn, hawthorn, and nonsuckering shrubs have not been able to reproduce. Every seedling has been devoured year after year by cows, sheep, and goats.

I drove past a feedlot for sheep once. The ground was churned to mud. Not a blade of grass—not a stalk of weed—could be seen anywhere. Even the tree bark had been consumed as high as the sheep could reach, killing the trees.

Overgrazing is not the only culprit. Long ago, plowing destroyed the prairie sod, allowing wind and rainstorms to erode the topsoils off of the fields. Rain water now runs off; it doesn't soak into aquifers, natural underground water storage areas that keep springs and creeks running when no rain has fallen for months. The entire natural cycle of the land and all of the life it supports is disturbed.

Wild fires used to sweep over the prairies. Naturally, no farmer or rancher wants to risk his crops, his house, and his barns. However, many studies have shown that little bluestem gets thick and covers the ground completely only when it is regularly burned.

Clearly, it isn't only outdated land-use laws that contribute to the degradation of the land. Our point of view is also flawed. We look at land as something to be consumed and exploited, not as a resource to be cherished for the long haul.

Recently, those two ranches came back to me forcibly, when I heard one of those one-minute inspirational messages on the radio. This one really hit home, and I want to share some of what I heard with you. The message was called "Species Pride," and it was delivered by the Reverend Hal Brady, Pastor of Dallas's First United Methodist Church. Brady reminded us that "of all our sins and shortcomings . . . species pride is the one most frequently ignored. The sin of species pride is when we humans become arrogant in our human-centeredness. In relation to plants, animals, the earth, the environment, and the rest of creation, we place an overemphasis on *dominion* and an underemphasis on the *interdependence of all created life.*"

Of course, it's not difficult to see how we got this way. First, we had biblical sanction. We were told clearly in Genesis that we were put here "to replenish the earth and subdue it." We're doing great on the subdue part, anyway.

Our forebears didn't see anything wrong with subduing and exploiting the earth. After all, there was plenty of everything around for everybody, and it was unimaginable to them that the vast forests might in fact be finite, that the mighty oceans might get gunked up with garbage and industrial waste. Brady concluded by saying, "Today, of course, we know better. . . ." Well, maybe. Some of us do, but too many members of our species still haven't got a clue. We elect a lot of them.

As for that land in the Hill Country near my friend's ranch . . . it may come back, but only if it is left alone. It doesn't have a good chance, unless we make it as financially attractive for landowners to conserve their land as despoil it.

Our plan to save our vanishing wildlands starts by having state legislatures recognize conservation as a valid land use, allowing landowners the same tax breaks for maintaining natural habitats that they receive for farming or ranching. In 1991, Texas took an encouraging step in that direction by passing a law that recognizes "wildlife management" as an "agricultural use." This is primarily to benefit those farmers and ranchers who lease out hunting rights, but many of our native habitats will benefit.

To help actively regenerate our native grasslands, the federal government has devised a plan, administered by county extension agents, to help working ranchers reseed with our native grasses, which are more nutritious.

Some studies are showing that a different regime of grazing—short-term followed by months of rest—actually increases grass productivity. And, controlled burning can be very beneficial to pastures.

Land conservation is not just a problem for rural communities. The preservation of our land, water, and wildlife is vital to all of us. It is important that we all learn about land management, and let our state representatives know how we feel.

Where Have All the Saplings Gone, Long Time Passing?

White Rock Lake is a very pleasant body of water in our neighborhood. It is home to water fowl, fish, at least one beaver, and—on the first warm weekend of spring—an army of riffraff and low lifes who play their car radios at ear-drum-breaking levels and then depart, leaving the lake ringed with empty beer cans, fried chicken boxes, and styrofoam cups.

The lake used to be far from the outskirts of town; it didn't move, Dallas did. Today, White Rock Lake is considered practically downtown. When it was dammed in the 1920s to become the water reservoir for the City of Dallas, the surrounding land became a park. For the last seventy years, its banks have been mowed by the Parks Department—except for where it's been so well-trod by fishermen and picnickers that there's nothing left to mow.

During that seventy years, the willows and cottonwoods have become huge and geriatric. The shorter-lived understory trees have died. As you stroll around the lakeshore, you can't help but notice that there are no seedlings, no saplings, no young trees at all. For seventy years, no young trees have been allowed to replace the aging giants. Now, the city must embark on a very expensive planting program. With a little forethought, this would not have been necessary.

In the Hill Country of central Texas, there are any number of farms and ranches where you can't find a tree that is younger than 100 years old. Huge lindens, cherries, live oaks, and post oaks dominate the scene. The only smaller trees I've seen in my survey of several ranches are Bigelow oak (called scrub oak) and rusty blackhaw viburnum (*V. rufidulum*). These trees are all exceptionally long-lived.

Why aren't there any babies to carry on the line? Why aren't there redbuds, sumacs, hercules clubs, or any other small trees so prevalent along the roadsides? For over one hundred years, something's been happening to all of the seedling trees.

In the Hill Country, they were gobbled up. In the early part of this century, farmers overstocked with sheep and goats; another drought followed. Both the land and the farmers have been trying to recover since then.

In an effort to save the livestock, ranchers declared open season on wolves, coyotes, and mountain lions. At the same time, the screwworm and other livestock parasites were brought under control. All of this fostered a proliferation of deer, who ate the seedlings.

I am especially concerned when I see post oak lands, where grazing or mowing prevent regeneration. Post oaks (*Quercus stellata*) are the principal canopy tree for an enormous portion of the United States. Traditionally, they grew in dry woodlands and savannahs (grasslands dotted with trees) bordering the lush eastern woods and the tall-grass prairies. When I hear doggerel about "mighty oaks," I immediately picture post oaks. These are big spreading trees with strong, gnarled limbs; there are no wimpy twigs. Periodic fires kept them spaced far apart allowing them to develop broad, spreading limbs. They form thick, corky bark to withstand these fires. They look burly and tough. But, as you'll soon see, that macho look is deceptive.

Most important, post oaks inhabit the poor soils where lower rainfall, fast drainage, and poor nutrient levels make it difficult for most other large trees to thrive. If post oaks disappeared, a large part of our native landscape would disappear along with them, to be replaced by less majestic trees such as bois d'arc, hackberry, locust, and blackjack oak.

As our urban sprawl covers post oak lands, the "mother" trees are being killed, usually by accident. These trees are very appealing, and homeowners and developers alike go to great lengths to save them. But like all trees, they are vulnerable to changes in ground level and having their bark torn up.

They are also extremely sensitive to cement, paint, and caustic chemicals.

However, post oaks have an extra sensitivity: The way it's been explained to me, post oak roots are stiff and stubby, and the hair roots that do the actual work are easily shifted when trucks run over them. Furthermore, they are accustomed to large amounts of oxygen in the soil. When the soil is compacted by construction and then overwatered by homeowners who put in thirsty plants that are mismatched with the original environment, the post oaks literally suffocate.

So, if you lose your mother post oak or never had one to begin with, can you just run out to the nearest nursery and buy another? Unfortunately, no. I haven't heard of any nursery owner currently growing post oaks.

But, according to Robert Vines, the author of *Trees, Shrubs and Woody Vines of the Southwest* (University of Texas Press, 1960), post oaks were grown commercially in 1819, and it really isn't too difficult. Their germination and growth rates are comparable to oaks being grown commercially today.

At this point, if you want a post oak, you have to hire your local tree-moving expert to transplant one from the wild (which doesn't exactly up the total number and requires landowner permission), or you have to go find your own acorn and plant it. This is true for many of our important indigenous trees.

Look around your neighborhood, wherever you live. If the trees are getting old and there are no youngsters to replace them, take action. One obvious, and easy, way to help tree seedlings get established is temporary fencing. Fencing keeps mowers or livestock from destroying all of the seedlings, allowing some to grow into saplings. When the saplings get old enough to be less vulnerable, remove the fencing and thin them out so they will not become overcrowded.

I'm sure there are other solutions, too. I recently read about four-foot-tall plastic tubes being used in Pekin, Illinois, to protect very young saplings from mowers and other urban hazards, such as rambunctious little boys.

There is a two-fold advantage in allowing your native trees to seed out. First, the costs are dramatically less than buying, planting, and watering nursery-grown trees. Second, instead of planting ill-adapted or environmentally harmful trees, you are preserving the very trees and gene pools that are tailor-made by Mother Nature for where you live.

To Save the Planet, Save the Plants

You've seen the bumper stickers: Save the Whales, Save the Tigers, Save the Elephants. It's scary how we're gradually—and in some cases, not so gradually—eliminating entire species of animals.

The case made by naturalists over and over again states that each one of these creatures is an important piece in the vast mosaic of life on our home planet. We are all interdependent; if we lose one species, it affects us all, perhaps in ways that we do not yet understand or appreciate.

As an animal lover, I am, of course, concerned. But, I'm also a plant lover, and I can't help but notice that an important part of the save the animals story is not being effectively told—specifically, that we cannot save these animals unless we also save their habitats. We can eliminate all of the ivory poaching, all of the whaling ships, all of the big-game sports hunters . . . and we would lose these creatures anyway.

Don't animal naturalists realize that plants are part of that mosaic? Those wild animals didn't evolve in zoos, eating baled hay or cat food, under plastic awnings for shelter. They grazed on prairies, browsed shrubs, and hunted herbivores. And they mated, rested, and nested in thickets, forests, prairies, and marshes—vegetational environments.

It is not enough that we recognize that individual animal species are threatened; we must appreciate the relationships that exist among *all* species, both animal and plant. They overlap and intertwine in ever-widening circles to ultimately encompass the whole earth.

Plant life supports animal life, but it works the other way, too; insects fertilize the flowers, and birds and mammals distribute the seeds that are not sown by the wind.

We're not talking about something that occurs only in distant and exotic lands. Here, at home, wolves, bears, and other native American animals are at risk of becoming zoological has-beens. And, that's because they are losing their native habitats. The trees and shrubs are dwindling. And with them the berries and mushrooms, and insects, birds, and rodents— all of which are a part of the support system that keeps bigger animals alive and fruitful.

Sometimes this strikes me as being so obvious that I feel self-conscious even going on like this. But then I look at how we are devastating *our* remnant native vegetation to support *African* refugee animals in wildlife parks.

And, I wonder, why we are clear-cutting our forests and replanting cash crops when selective cutting can provide timber and retain habitat? A plantation of pines is not a forest habitat. It is a sterile monoculture, without underbrush, berries, mushrooms, or varied native saplings growing up through the thick layers of pine needles. These tree plantations are unnaturally silent; the singing of birds is rarely heard here.

As we become more knowledgeable and environmentally sophisticated, we can support enlightened legislation and conservation efforts on a larger scale. Also, focus your attention closer to home. There is a great deal of satisfaction to be gained by doing something on your own. And, the most basic thing we can *all* do is to plant native trees, shrubs, flowers, and grasses in our home gardens.

Sure, I know it won't keep mountain lions and herds of buffalo alive, but it can make a big difference for songbirds, butterflies, bees, and hawk moths. Then, imagine what could happen if all of your neighbors did the same thing.

When natural landscapes are used on larger pieces of property, in conjunction with creeks or ponds, they become habitats that can attract and support larger wildlife such as owls, hawks, raccoons, opossums, and foxes. These animals are not dangerous to humans; we have been dangerous to them. Given the chance, they can live very peaceably in close proximity to us. Remember, good neighbors come in all species.

We need to save parcels out of development tracts—natural green spaces that can serve as havens for wildlife. We need to replant existing but barren parks. On these larger plots, we can preserve a much greater diversity of native plants than would be suitable for typical urban gardens. Wildflowers, rampant berry bushes, tangles, and thickets vital for nesting birds would flourish in these places. Here, too, we would we see rotting logs that are vital to the life cycles of far more creatures than we realize.

It's easier to have a say in your county or city affairs if you belong to some organization. Most states have native plant societies, wildflower clubs, or prairie associations. These groups dispense information, hold field trips and lectures, plant gardens, and help maintain preserves.

If I've whetted your interest, and you want to know where to find such a group near you, get a copy of *The National Wildflower Research Center's Wildflower Handbook*. This is an invaluable guide to organizations and people, nurseries and books. There is a state-by-state listing of nature preserves, arboretums that feature native plants, conservation and native plant societies, local Nature Conservancy offices, native plant nurseries, landscape designers and architects, and other useful people, organizations, and public places that help you locate information about the native plants of your area.

If you can't find a copy in your bookstore or library, write to The National Wildflower Research Center, 2600 FM 973 North, Austin, Texas, 78725-9990.

We haven't the time to take our time.

E U G E N E   I O N E S C O

Although we've covered a lot of ground in these pages, I feel as if I've barely scratched the surface. Hardly a day goes by when I don't learn something new and exciting about native plants—usually from observing them in the wild, often from lay gardeners like you who were just messing around in their own gardens and learned what a certain plant will or won't do.

Native plant landscaping, to my mind, is going to have as profoundly positive an effect on our gardens and our environment as our new and enlightened ideas on nutrition are having on our health. Using native plants is far more than just another way to make your garden look pretty—it actually has the potential to change the world for the better. And how many things can you say that about these days?